# JOURNEY OF THE SELF

# JOURNEY
## OF THE SELF

## AS SEEN THROUGH THE EYES OF GOD

Recorded as received from her guide, Mother.
By
Judith

**BALBOA**
PRESS

A DIVISION OF HAY HOUSE

Balboa Press books may be ordered through booksellers or by contacting:

Balboa Press
A Division of Hay House
1663 Liberty Drive
Bloomington, IN 47403
www.balboapress.com
1 (877) 407-4847

Cover image is the Helix Nebula - NGC 7293
Hubble Space Telescope - Advanced Camera for Surveys
NOAO 0.9m - Mosaic 1 Camera
NASA, NOAO, ESA, The Hubble Helix Team,
M. Meixner (STScl), and T.A. Rector (NRAO) - STScl- PRC03-11a

ISBN: 978-1-4525-9102-5 (e)
ISBN: 978-1-4525-9101-8 (sc)

Printed in the United States of America.

Balboa Press rev. date: 2/7/2014

## DEDICATION

For you Dad, throughout my life you were always there with your love and support. And I was honored to be there for you when you passed.

This one's for you.

# CONTENTS

# ACKNOWLEDGMENTS

This book wouldn't have had a chance had it not been for the support, dedication and expert editing of my friend Dorine Owens. She picked me up when I faltered, laughed with me when we were dizzy from rewrites and slapped me around when I needed it. For Marla, who rightfully called me the *comma queen*, I am forever in your debt and any extra commas are totally on me. Last, but definitely not least, a big hug and thank you to my husband for all his patience, encouragement and support. You made it all possible.

To my guide and true author of this book, Mother, I give my most humble and heartfelt love and appreciation for her patience, humor, love and guidance along my path and personal journey of the Self. And to all the guides and teachers I have had the privilege to meet along the way; mere words cannot express what you have meant to me.

# THE AWAKENING SPIRIT

It is the dry season in Peru and as I climb down among the massive boulders and jagged rocks to sit beside the rushing water of the Urubamba River, the sun warms my back. At the water's edge, the sound is deafening and pulsating with life. With utter fascination I watch this liquid movement as it shapes the rocks from years of devotion to its journey downstream and to its single purpose—the merging with the one true source, the ocean. All intent, all energy, all movement is focused on one objective: to return to the source. Along the way, while cascading through the land, some liquid is taken up and some is added, but the journey's motivation remains the same—to connect to source.

On this earthly plane of existence, man and woman have a similar journey, a similar focus. We are forever moving toward the One Source, our God, and we travel many diverse paths to get there. Some leave before the merging is complete, so they return to journey once more. We are much like this river—churning, swirling and shaping our existence from lifetimes of dedication and commitment to return to the Source. This separation from Source is only an illusion, a dream that is played out in various scenarios and on many stages. Still, it is a fantasy of our own choosing. Why not play it out the best we can, with joy and without judgment? Only then can we sit by the river, watch it flow and be at peace with the beauty of life and the creation brought forth through our eternal connection to God.

A small, white butterfly catches my eye as I begin to remember the events in my life that brought me to this moment's contemplation in this magical land called Peru. I was introduced to my spiritual studies by my younger sister in 1980 through some past-life hypnosis sessions. I soon became hooked and thoroughly intrigued by all things spiritual. I devoured books by Ruth Montgomery and Edgar Cayce and many such authors of spirit. I haunted the "New Age" section of bookstores, at times feeling as if I was falling down Alice's rabbit hole. My life continued to unfold, and during the ensuing years I spent a good deal of time exploring the world of spirit. I had several channeled readings, went to Psychic Fairs, had my astrological chart done and my palm read. It was all so incredibly fascinating that I virtually became a spiritual junkie! It was great fun, and I believed absolutely everything these psychic wonders told me. How could they know I was so wonderful and bound for such great adventures? How could they see all those beautiful colors around me, and know who I had been in past lives and what I would be in the future just from checking the planets and stars in the universe and the lines on my hand? Oh, the wonder and the mysteries I had yet to explore! For me it was a very exciting time.

In the summer of 1986, I had the opportunity to go with some friends to experience a young woman who channeled an Ascended Master. She was described as a full-body channel that leaves the body completely so that this Illumed Master could take over and speak without the interference of the human channel's ego mind. (It is similar to the experience of the channel J.Z. Knight and her guide Ramtha.) It was a warm evening in July when I joined a group of about fifty curious people to listen to this Ascended Master's teaching. He spoke for over an hour and his message was one of love and recognition that we were all Gods. He talked about our chakra centers, helped us to open them and spoke of the powers and properties of crystals. This teacher was very gentle, loving and kind, and was soon to become a very important influence in my life as an evolving spiritualist. My experience with this Master and his teachings helped to set me on a journey that continues to this day. He opened many doors for me and I had incredible awakenings each time I was in his presence. I studied with him on and off for many years. He told me from the first day that it was not my journey to continually be in his presence but "let me be your well and drink from the well, but march more than you drink." So I did.

I would go, learn what he had to teach me and then go into the world to live the wisdom and attempt to teach it by how I lived.

A few weeks later, I was given an opportunity to take an eight-week channeling class from this same teacher. He began our first week's meeting by discussing the serious nature of channeling that it was not a game to be taken lightly. He spoke of the good that channeling does by raising our own vibrational level, as well as others, within this energy field and the world as a whole. The group that had gathered in the class was told to consider what effect channeling would have on us physically. As our electrum (the vibrational energy field) in our body increased, we needed to remember to eat only good, wholesome food that would not disturb our digestion. He explained that if we chose to eat the meat from slaughtered animals, we should know that it carried with it the memory of the traumatic death it suffered and that this trauma would, in turn, be transferred to our cellular memory when we ingested it. We were cautioned to get plenty of rest and to channel only those entities from the highest dimensions. He also spoke about the effect the raised energy would have on our fears. Everything that was not working in our lives at the time would be magnified. He said that if we did not face our fears and relinquish them in the dream state or in meditation, we would manifest them in the physical.

That first night he asked us to close our eyes as he led us through a meditation, and then began to help each of us individually to channel the beings that were here to guide us. I remember sitting quietly with my eyes closed, enjoying the peaceful ebb and flow of the energy surrounding me, as this teacher went from student to student to assist them. Then through my closed eyelids, I saw the teacher's light as he approached me. He gently touched my third eye chakra (located between the eyebrows and up a bit) and had me speak the name of the guide who was with me. In a timid whisper I spoke the name "Joseph," an entity who would soon become known to me as Ezekiel, my first significant guide. He was with me in spirit connection for more than twenty years, and helped prepare me for my next guide and the true author of this book, Mother.

From the time I first began to meditate and then to channel, I have listened in the stillness and experienced a quiet knowing. I cannot, in all fairness, call it a voice separate from mine; it's more a knowing with a mind of its own. This knowing comes to me in several ways. Sometimes I am taken on a journey of sensation that weaves colors, sights and sounds into a tapestry of experience attached to a message. At other times, this knowing presents itself as a rather self-assured presence with answers to questions and specific teachings that are profound, often humorous, and, at the same time, incredibly enlightening. After transcribing the teachings of Ezekiel over the years and now Mother, I have come to the conclusion that our answers are all there, if we just take the time to sit quietly and listen to that still, small voice within.

My journey continues with the past weaving into the present and the present moving without end into the future. I have traveled several times to the land of Peru where I had the opportunity to experience some very significant transformations. Each trip was a step closer to my knowledge of the Self and the realization of my life's purpose. I was continually being guided in new directions to experience further revelations and connections to spirit that would begin to expand my horizons in incredible ways. My job was to surrender to what was inevitable, and I realized this surrender had been planned from the beginning of time.

On the day before my birthday, I was shopping in one of my favorite metaphysical stores filled with a variety of unique items, when I saw a sign over the door to a small room in the back of the shop that read "Tarot Card Readings." I couldn't resist, and on the spur of the moment I decided to have a reading. I found the Tarot card reader to be a delightful woman about my age with a special gift that she willingly shares with the world. Many seek her council, and I found myself quite happy to sit with her in her beautiful room at the back of this busy, bustling store. After I settled in a chair across the table from her, she began our session with a prayer for divine guidance and highest wisdom. I touched the Tarot cards with my right hand, and then she shuffled and spread them face-down on the table in front of me. I was asked to pick ten cards from this spread and to stack them face-down before her. She turned them over slowly, one by one, giving each a moment's contemplation before she spoke. What she said seemed to have very little to do with the cards in front of her and everything to do with what she was receiving from the guides who were present around me. As her eyes focused slightly off to my left, she spoke about the messages and visions she was receiving. The information was unusually vague, which seemed to trouble her greatly. When she asked the guides to elaborate, they wouldn't clarify their answers. She kept repeating the only thing they would tell her—that I would be receiving ancient wisdom very soon, and that it looked as if it was coming from somewhere out in the universe, not of this earth. The guides wouldn't give her anything more.

I left the session more than a little confused, but I really didn't give it too much thought as I went on with daily life. Work and family consumed much of my time, and the weeks passed with little thought or reflection on what she had shared with me. About two months later, I walked back into the store and saw this same woman standing quietly by the counter. She looked as if she had been waiting for me. She smiled in recognition, and on impulse, I decided to see what her cards had to show me that day.

Before I settled myself in her room, I jokingly remarked that since our last session I hadn't received any information, ancient or new, from any unseen forces. But as soon as the words left my mouth, I remembered my dream from the night before. In this dream, I had experienced a powerful female presence superimposed over and around my body in what felt like a very intense, loving hug. I hadn't remembered this dream until the moment I sat down. She began the reading and, with a quiet dignified grace, introduced me to the guide I know now as Mother. She saw her body clearly superimposed over mine. I could feel the intensity of Mother's presence and recognized it as the same sensation I had felt in my dream the night before.

> "A very ancient woman with flowing, white hair is showing herself to me very clearly. I can see her face, and she seems alive to me. The images I am picking up are very clear. She is overlaying you."

I asked if she was the one in my dream the night before.

> "Yes. Definitely. She brings very ancient wisdom. That is what she is calling it, ancient wisdom. They are already working with you to open more your crown chakra."

As she continued talking, I began to experience insights and memories related to my connection with this ancient one, whom she described as similar to a high priestess.

> "I knew her before, in my lifetime in Lemuria, didn't I? We've worked together before," I said.

She confirmed this.

> "Yes. Yes. You have worked together before. She has a lot of information, and you are basically here helping to get it out to the physical world at this point in time. This is something that is very high-end and it makes a lot of sense, but is not utilized or known at this time."

The memories of our time together were coming to me in rapid succession and vivid detail. I explained to her that this ancient one and I were members of a sect that embedded crystals within the interior walls of select pyramids scattered across the world, but that they were not those now found in Egypt. I remembered that the top of these pyramids could actually open, and when the sun shone down inside them, it would set off a visual light display of the crystals. People who stood inside the pyramids, in the reflection of the rainbow colors cast by the linking of the sun and crystals, would be healed. I could see it as clearly as I could see the woman sitting across from me. As she spoke, memories of my connection to this ancient one continued to surface.

> "She taught me how to use the crystals," I said.

> "She has taught you quite a bit."

And then I knew.

> "I called her Mother, didn't I?"

> "She wasn't your mother, but you called her that. You lived with her, and you were in training—like an apprentice. She showed you everything. They are showing me that she took you out

to a dry river bed where you collected materials for a healing ceremony. It was very rocky. The stones were white. She was telling you what these various items were for and why you had to collect them. You were very young. In this desert land, she had a tent-like structure made of white cloth with an opening in the front but closed on all sides. You were seated on the ground outside off to one side, sorting the collection of rocks from your previous exploration. You were laying them out in some kind of pattern while she remained inside. A woman had come to Mother for healing. Later, when the woman came out, she was crying and holding an oval-shaped stone that was dark on the outside with green running through the center. You observed the woman crying, and it bothered you greatly. The woman left and Mother came over to you and took the opportunity to explain what had happened. I don't know if this woman was cured or not."

I said, "Sometimes they can't be," and I remembered it all.

The following day, after my reading, I sat down at my computer and began receiving my first message from the ancient one whom I call Mother. I felt her energy surround me as I quietly placed myself in front of the computer. My hands felt heavy and solid upon the keyboard. The intensity of her essence and presence mirrored my dream-like experience. I closed my eyes and gave myself over to the experience of transcribing her first message to me. I was completely conscious but in a somewhat altered state.

"While we are accessing your body and mind as a conduit to our messages and adjusting the ebb and flow of our message, you will be feeling a bit of pressure throughout your body. Adjust the speed of your typing and you will not make as many mistakes as you are afraid of. We are in no hurry. Our time together will be lengthy, and you will be improving as we go along. Your belief in what is occurring for you right now, or your attention to the overall feel of your body tension and heaviness, will be abbreviated in the future."

The words continued to flow onto the page, and when the message was complete, the feeling of gentle pressure left me and I could once again move freely. For the rest of the day, I was shaky and a little queasy from the intense energy that had briefly found me functioning between worlds.

The next morning I awoke at 4:00 AM, eyes wide open and ready to begin the process once again. The energy was different this time—less intense and extreme. Mother said that in deference to my workday, her presence would be gentler but the message just as accurate. She said we were "practicing" together. I was practicing to give up control and to allow the messages to come freely without ego interference, and she was gauging the level of energy I could handle.

> "Adjustments are being made. Quiet yourself. The evolution of the soul is such that it may yet take a few minutes of breathing and emptying the mind before you are ready to receive. Quiet yourself and accept that you will not be late for work."

The following morning, I awoke at 4:00 AM once again to receive her message. While at work later that same day, I experienced a burning sensation starting in the center of my chest and exiting straight through to my back, in the area of my heart chakra. It was most uncomfortable, and I experienced this sensation on and off throughout the day. Though it was rather painful, I knew it had something to do with the energy I was receiving. That night, after going to sleep and about an hour into deep slumber, I woke up with a start. It felt as if someone had pulled a plug in the center of my chest. For a brief moment, I felt violently ill. But just as rapidly as it had come, this feeling passed with no lasting effect, and I went back to sleep. The next day, the burning sensation in the area of my heart was gone. I accepted this occurrence as being part of the adjustment process and knew it was an important opening of my heart center to better receive her information.

Daily, for over six months, I maintained this rhythm of waking in the early morning, transcribing Mother's messages, going to work, tending to family and earthly matters, falling asleep and waking to start the process all over again. After many months of early-morning dictation and hundreds of pages of text later, Mother spoke to me one morning before I was fully awake.

"It's about the words," she whispered. "It's always about the words."

My eyes flew open as I stumbled from my bed.

"What do you mean, I asked?"

"It's about the words," she said.

It seemed Mother was trying to access my stubborn and often resistant conscious mind while I was half awake.

"It's about the words," she repeated.

Then I realized what she was trying to tell me. And it was in this knowing that the connection was made. I began to understand that it was not only the words that are literally recorded on each page but the way in which the words fit together that carried the vibrational energy of truth. It is about the words. But at the same time, I am being asked to look beyond their literal meaning and open to the way in which they flow together as a whole. She had given me this insight because I often found transcribing her messages frustrating and my vocabulary too limited to convey the true meaning I sensed was there. Each day I would listen to her words, type what I was given and then read over what I had transcribed. I would often feel disappointed in my ability to convey the essence of her words accurately. At times, I would even stop the flow of the message in frustration, and the morning's session would instead become a lesson in allowing the words to come as given, without judgment or censorship of any kind. She spoke to me about my frustration one morning:

> Do not be disappointed as to what is expressed. The words are limited only by your judgment of the outcome on the page. The words are given to you in such a manner as to set off avenues of learning heretofore unknown and unrealized. Upon reading a transcribed passage, you often say "I don't understand." And it is so. You do not understand because to equate the words with their true meaning takes practice. And so we continue to practice

until such time as you see between the lines of text unto a greater understanding of the Self as a whole being.

And so it is with great honor and humility that I present the messages as they were given to me from the one I call Mother and recorded as faithfully as possible. I hope that you will know of what she speaks when she says, "It is about the words," and that you listen with an open heart and receive the true meaning found between these lines of text. It is a journey I happily continue to this day.

~Namaste~

Judith

# CHAPTER ONE

# OUR JOURNEY BEGINS

I am the one from the ancient past now known to you as Mother. I have been observing your spiritual evolution throughout this lifetime and have stepped in now because you are ready to have us meet once again. Our reunion yesterday was destined to be. The woman who introduced us aptly described me as "ancient." I appeared as a person with flowing white hair and wizened face to emphasize that I am from a very ancient culture, far older than your recorded history.

When I first came to you on this earth plane, you were as a daughter to me—though, in actuality, you were not of my genetic blood. Our time together then was to prepare you for what is occurring now during the earth's present evolution. I was not of this earth then, nor am I now. However, for the purpose of teaching you the wonders of what had yet to be brought to this planet, you were given to me as a child, very young indeed—only four of your earth years. I was ancient to you even then, with white hair and wrinkled face. I came to teach you. As you were my only pupil, you called me Mother and continued to do so as we journeyed together. We came to the land known as Persia and lived out from the towns and villages. We created a temple of comfort for our stay, as we were able to do this quite easily then. In this temple, I began to teach you some of the things that would be important for you to know when next we would meet, during this current lifetime. We practiced in Persia, in our temple that housed many ancient ones, and you grew in the knowledge. You have not been to this planet often; however, you did come here during the time of Jesus and a few lifetimes before then. You also stayed away for long periods of time while living out trainings and initiations on other levels of existence.

Why am I sharing this with you now? So you will know that this has all been preparation for what is occurring at this time. You have been in a universal school preparing for now. You have had your few lifetimes only to experience the love of human-to-human as partner and parent, in order to round out your experience. We all have a job to do, and yours is to record the teachings as they are given. Your home, the one you long for, is the universal one which you will understand as we proceed. For now, it is enough to practice and get back in the habit of listening and recording. You have waited and you have prepared; now just do it. I know that I may sound impatient or unhappy with you, but it is not true. That is your ego judgment speaking out. You must practice letting that go. You are loved and honored in the universal community. We love your courage and dedication. You are a student always but are now beginning to take on the role of the mother who nurtures the Soul, is the healer of mind and body, and one who frees the Soul to journey another reality. It is how you gain your prominence. The one who stands on your left, the blue ray known to you as Ezekiel, is always with you. I am Mother, and you are my student for now. Acknowledge the light of our loving presence and be glad. The information will come. You are not to force it. We are pleased that you have placed yourself here at this time. Now you must open more to our energy.

Walk with me back to the time when creatures roamed the earth, back to the awakening Spirit that began on this earth in earnest over billions—yes, billions—of years ago. Those who had come to create new wonders had begun to populate the earth and were evolving rapidly. A species would pop up here and there, disappear, reappear and stay or leave as the thought processes of the creators were refined. This is how the planets were populated billions of years ago as we traveled around the universes. And, yes, there is more than one universe. They are as infinite as the one God is infinite. This experiment on planet earth was your true beginning. It came in stages, in which we would populate, experiment and then leave. You were among those who experimented but never stayed long. Life was formed from your thoughts and creative ability, for everything was possible. Our intentions were pure, though at times we did get carried away a bit. But that is how you learn, correct? Create, experiment and then refine what you intend. It was a playful time. It was a serious time. And it was a time of great learning.

We enjoyed our moments here, but we never became so enmeshed in this planet called earth that we were motivated to make it our permanent home. For some it became their Eden, and they stayed to populate and experience that which is called "human form." Life on this planet became a trap. Forgetting their God-Self created heaviness within the hearts of some. But then that is why they stayed—for the experience. What I speak of occurred billions of years ago and was never recorded. We built a beautiful trap. We dug a comfortable hole and have been climbing out ever since. Oh, what a journey this experiment has been! Did you know that the earth has had a variety of inhabitants of every shape and form before this present manifestation? Experimentation took place over thousands of years, and when we created something that didn't work, it was quickly gone. This is how we learned—much like a baby who toddles to the hot stove and has to get burned only once to realize the folly.

Why am I going on about something that will not matter in the long run? You and I are practicing with the flow of information and our alignment together. We are practicing much like those who have gone before us. It is good for you to remove your conscious mind, be at peace with the process and know that time can stand still if you wish it to. Until we have your complete focus, we will practice thusly. These are your first toddling steps in learning to trust.

*In the early morning hours, when I would sit and listen to Mother's words spoken not as a separate voice but one that lived within me, I often contemplated what I was here to accomplish. The doubts would come to the surface, and I would feel my interference with the flow of information and the message being shared. Mother would then speak to me about my doubts and fears in an attempt to quiet my troubled mind.*

I hear your prayers, and I am here to answer them and to bring you the peace that has so far eluded you. This candle that I have asked you to light represents the Oneness of it all. You see not two or three flames but only one. Understand? You are still my daughter, yet separate from me in many ways. It is how our story begins. We are separate and yet one. It is one of the first lessons you were taught as my young pupil. I would hold you on my knee and sing to you of heaven. I would sing to you of worlds unknown, yet ancient and all-knowing. I would sing to you of futures yet to come, and then you would sleep to dream of all possibilities. The memories are beginning to come to you in waves. I have sent them to you for many more years than you realize. I will tell you, the temple you remembered from your first lifetime in Peru was a temple we inhabited for many years. At that time, we could change it at will to suit our purpose. Today this would be called "magic" and the word would be quietly spoken, but at that time it was commonplace for us to do so—that is, change anything and everything at will, our will.

I will bring back to you the memory of a temple that we had placed in ancient Peru before it was called by that name. Do you remember? The mountains were beautiful and very sacred. Gods lived there. Truly, Gods lived there. And the people who came to inhabit this land came from the caves in the mountains that housed these Gods. Our temple at the base of these mountains and on the flat of the land received the people when they came to earth, where we refined their vibrational frequency so they could acclimate to the Earth's surface, which was still boiling and shifting in some places. I am speaking of ancient, ancient times, before your Bible's Adam and Eve. Your planet was continuing to evolve into the beautiful land it has since become. The earth, as Soul, is forever changing and shifting and evolving.

The earth doesn't look anything like it did when first we came to inhabit it. It was a landscape of flat spaces; rather dry and dusty. Rain was brought to feed the land because we remembered rain from whence we came. We brought forth the seeds from other lands; some we created from memory. It was a time of joyful creation. We placed our temple there on the flat of the land below the mountains, and we received all the people. Because it is important to our current message and its reception, I will tell you that our temple was set with crystals brought from other universes. Some are still buried there on this land. The crystals were quite large, and we placed them in a semi-circle with an opening to the east. These crystals were aligned in such a way that when the sun rose to full expression, the light created would spark and leap from mountain peak to mountain peak. The people traveled from the mountains toward this beacon of light, for this was something they remembered. Then they would walk through the crystalline portal and step up into a narrow, rectangular room with large columns running along both sides, supporting the roof and leading to a semi-solid wall in the back. They walked through the center of this room to the far wall that surrounded a large, round suspended disk made of transparent material. This material is not presently known because, in actuality, it had been created for just this purpose. This disk was rimmed in a brilliant gold, while the materials in the center shimmered and sparked with energy and luminescent light. The disk was quite large—ten of your feet in diameter—but those who arrived were also quite tall, so it didn't seem quite so immense to them.

At the time, you were around ten of your years—quite young, though very accomplished in the ways I have shared with you. We stood on either side of this suspended circle of gold. The people walked in flowing lines from the caves in the mountains to this temple on the flat of the land and were assisted by the two of us to move through this shimmering disk that vibrated at such an accelerated rate that one could only slip through it by breathing in synchronicity with its vibrational pulse. The final step in determining their ability to survive on this land called planet earth occurred when they were able to pass in between the vibrating molecules and through the disk safely.

We have now begun to overlay you with many memories all at once and to speak with you of things that seem beyond belief. We want you to practice acceptance for the future information that will seem to make perfect sense while, at the same time, be too outrageous to believe. Write it all down. Only in this way will you learn to accept what must be written and shared for future times. We are pleased with the determination you have shown transcribing the material and with the sight of you in this early morning quiet time.

Now open your eyes and edit at will. Go forth unto your day, daughter mine. Go forth. You have served us well in this morning tide. We are smiling, and we place the golden disk upon your soul, covering your heart and throat centers. All who come upon you will be at peace this day. Your vibrational flow is altered ever so slightly to accommodate this projection of vibrational pulse. You do not have to do anything. Just be and go forth unto your day in peace. Remember this temple and the passing through into all possibilities. It is now, at this time, that this door of all possibilities opens. Let the acceptance begin here, during this morning time of peace and quiet. Let it begin here.

One day you will sit upon this chair and the words will flow uncensored by your conscious mind, and you will be free of all doubt. I do not recognize the doubt that you have at this time but see only the daughter of my temple, whom I raised to become a teacher and healer, and a bringer of wisdom beyond the knowledge that is available at this time of the earth's evolution. Everything that we do now is in preparation for the eventuality of releasing once again the information that will assist humankind to go forth and to move out of the density that has been created from forgetfulness.

Your expression of doubt will serve as a perfect example for the rest of mankind. Doubt fills the souls of humans as they move further and further into density, and they become blinded to moments of insight when the seemingly unexplainable occurs. I have watched it happen many, many times. Throughout the ages, there have been Souls who have remembered, risen up and moved beyond this limitation. You were one who was able to observe, move through doubt and help the evolving earth come to fruition.

Let me tell you of you, for your story is the story of many. Though you were brought forth to work with me in the various temples we initiated and to learn from my tutelage, you were not of this earth. You have come once more to be within this earthly dimension and herald a new time. You are not the only one here with this purpose, but you are the only one who is my pupil for now. You and I have a history together. We have a mission to accomplish and a promise to fulfill. We are going to join together with many light beings around the world to pull this human existence up by its bootstraps, to use a current expression.

I have observed for many centuries what has been occurring here. The varied expressions of humankind and their creations are never boring. Now come with me, daughter, and explore the depths of remembering that are just now beginning to occur in the hearts and minds of those beings that are awakening to yet another way of existence. It is not the way of the Christian, the Buddhist, the Hindu, the Jew, the Muslim or any other religious sect now practicing. It is not even the way of many of your enlightened teachers. But it is the way of the evolution of the Soul and the freedom of the Spirit, to soar into realms of awareness that were never known here on earth and only hinted at by those who ventured forth from other dimensions and told the stories of the ages. You have entered a time of magic and a period of timeless wisdom. It is the time of Original Thought personified. The words "original thought" are powerful indeed and will be the cornerstone on which we build our temple once more. Original thought is the center.

You have asked, "When does it end? When can I go home and rest? When is it over?" I say to you, not until all become original thought once more, and then it will start again. I know, daughter, it is not so clear now. You continue to be restricted by your conscious mind and find it difficult to comprehend something that is incomprehensible to those who only possess limited thinking. It is a seed I have planted, only a seed. But it is enough that you are stretching your mind in order to know and to understand that you must trust what is coming, what has been and what shall ever be. With discipline, we will take it one step at a time. Do not become frightened. Breathe and come to know your higher Self—your Original Thought—and be glad.

Walk quietly between the lines, as I have cautioned you to do this early morning hour. You have heard the words but have yet to truly understand them. When I ask you to "walk between the lines," it is for the purpose of using your ability to suspend time and harken to another way of being, rather than continue to think of yourself as a limited human. Walking quietly between the lines frees you to move between those lines of judgment that you find so rigid. These are the lines of thinking that keep you bound to the belief that this dimensional existence is all that there is. When you walk between the lines of which I speak, you definitely break with the boundaries that have kept you planted firmly within this limited realm of existence.

Walk with me and let us slip between this third dimensional reality and move into the reality that is you and me. We will not speak of things you are yet unable or unwilling to bring forth. We are still meeting and adjusting to your fear and resistance. This is why I have given you this lesson today, to help move you beyond this state of fear and resistance and into a "state of all possibility." Vibrating within the electrum that is human existence, you will see only what your senses tell you is real—what you can see, touch, taste, feel and hear. And then one day you will *know*. The *knowing* is the sense that has been developed in you and many others of your kind throughout this lifetime. The knowing will set you on the road to walking between realities, or, as I have termed them to be, your "lines or boundaries." You have always known and felt with more than so-called "reality" as your bellwether. You have practiced the knowing throughout this lifetime and many lifetimes yet realized. The knowing has set you apart. Many have this skill (I call it a "skill"), as they have honed it to perfection throughout the ages.

So walk with me now in this state of knowing that enables you to press your fingers upon these keys, keep your eyes closed and transcribe what you know to be true. In this state of knowing, all will become clear to you—clearer than if I were to appear and talk with you in human form. Through the knowing, we are going to teach you to walk between the realities of time and space and live with the gods, so to speak, and walk with the gods and meet them—not in this third-dimensional world but on the ground they walk, which in our reality is not ground at all. We will teach you there. When you were dedicated to meditating, you touched some of these places—albeit with judgment—but still you wrote them down and lived the memory. Do you see now how long you have been preparing for this moment? You have been preparing virtually all your life—all of your many lives. The task ahead of us will call for you to walk with ease between the lines and boundaries of our worlds, and to take what is given and use it for greater good.

There is so much for you to see and do. For those beings who will also experience the same set of realities and experiences as you, know it is what you have all come to do at this time. You will meet together at some point, but for now each of you will walk the path that is being guided by your willingness to arise each morning and face the challenge of letting go of conscious awareness and explore the possibilities of other realities yet unknown. You are in training. You are the scribe for this journey, and through your writing you will chronicle the experiences that will become the history for future travelers who have the courage to walk between the lines. Your planet will not self-destruct, though many now living upon it are bound to attempt it. It will not happen because it cannot be destroyed by ignorance. Ignorance is always foreshadowed by truth, and truth will always win out.

So, my daughter, our journey continues and yet begins upon a new frontier that is really older than the ages of recorded history. Magic is in the air surrounding you. Move through the boundaries of your existence and you will see the vista of all possibility laid out before you. These vibrational signposts are like open portals. Step through one and experience what is there, then look toward the next and move through and feel the wind upon your face that will tell your human mind that this is the reality you seek. Each boundary crossed and each line moved between will free you to open more fully and increase the vibrational flow that is growing and emanating from within you. Do not be afraid that you will lose yourself in the process. When you increase your awareness of limitless space and time—limitless possibilities—you can change at will what does not serve you. I know it may seem a most fantastic concept, but the seeds are being planted now. You are nurturing each seed carefully by writing and transcribing words upon the page each morning and moving with me as your guide and teacher through many realities. As a result, you will also be leaving behind the judgments that serve only to delay your process. You will never lose touch with your so-called reality here because of your promise to come and to teach, but it will not keep you from all possibility, for I will see that you remember. The promise you made to serve in this way was made many eons ago. We know that you have much you feel you must do, and places and people who call to you in this reality. You will find your balance, and those around you will grow as well. You must plant the seeds.

Be in joy, for it is a joyful time. Hear our song and sing it gladly. Feel the vibrational tones that blend the realities until no boundaries exist—limitless truth; all knowing; all seeing; all that there is. And still you will come upon another door that has never been opened, and it will present itself before you. And you will open this one too, and we will walk hand-in-hand and be teacher and student once more. But who shall be the teacher and who shall be the student? That will be the delightful question we will answer in some future time that is really not time at all. Is this not a wonderful thing to look forward to? Go forth and be happy, and let this be our greatest reward.

# CHAPTER TWO

# COME FORTH INTO THE ACT OF BEING

*Oftentimes, at the most unexpected moments, while taking a shower or brushing my teeth, I would receive a simple one-line message that was repeated over and over in my mind until I would finally stop and write it down. I have come to recognize these opportunities, which seem to come when least expected, as a clever way in which Mother would tweak my mind a bit and start me questioning and contemplating new directions in thought. This was one such occasion....*

So, have you been contemplating the messages from the shower of yester eve and now realize that nothing is given unto you that is without significance? When I gave you the message, *Think with limited thought*, you at once perceived this to be contradictory to all you had ever been taught. The very nature of that expression made you question the totality of your beliefs and years of spiritual study. This phrase was presented in this way for exactly that very reason. For far too long you have been receiving contradictory messages from many spiritual teachers, and it is my purpose to dismiss these teachings of the past until you have come once again before me as a "clean slate." I want you to realize that messages of those masters served a purpose at the time they were given. It was your job to carefully select the wisdom you felt true in that moment and keep moving forward.

We have watched you for a very long time and are not as out of touch as you might think.

Do you remember the next phrase that was given to you at the same time? It was the phrase that, for you, captures all meaning. It was: *Come forth into the act of being.* Quite simple, is it not? Truth always is. "Come forth" means to bring the Who that you are, the What that you are and the How that you are housed in this human shell. Come forth into the act of being. Come forth to what you are in truth—the truth that has never changed, has never altered, has never hidden, has always been correct and perfect in any form—and join with what you have *come forth to be.* This is your story now and has always been what you are about. Isn't it beautiful in its simplicity? *Come forth into the act of being.* I could dwell on this point and go into all the misconceptions that have occurred throughout the ages—all the half-truths and innuendos—but that would bring us into an altogether different "act of being," and I think you have wasted far too much time in that arena as it is. It is my purpose to bring you forth in the truth that has been constant from the beginning; the simple, direct and complete truth.

*Halfway into the transcription of this message, I created a distraction for myself and had to get up from the computer and leave for a few minutes. When I returned, I was given the opportunity to acknowledge a lesson in limited thought, which I received with more than a little chagrin.*

You have just been allowed to create your distraction to give you an example of *limited thought.* This morning you arose late and decided that the timing was not correct to receive my words… "limited thought." Then you hesitated in typing the transcription and felt like deleting all that had been given… limited thought. You went on to create a distraction and erroneously judged that you were correct about the poor timing of this message and once again experienced limited thought. Stopping and starting. Hesitation. Judgment. Fear. Disappointment. Congratulations, you have just created your day! I am still here observing and commenting on these events so you may see what your limited thought created when confronted with a simple message of truth. When we speak of the truths that are brought forth to replace your limited thought, we are able to remove the walls of deceit produced in the mind. And it is deceit, for limited thought has robbed you of your rightful place among the gods who watch over you, until you can once more come to your senses. Limited thought is an insidious disease that robs you of your Godhood.

There is a popular phrase used here on your planet that is very appropriate and speaks to my point: "Think outside the box." Where do you think the idea for this wonderful concept came from? It is a direct result of mankind's determination to come forth into the act of being, rather than from limited thought. This thoughtful phrase was given to the world by someone who escaped, for just one moment in time, the limited thought perpetuated by the conscious mind and then dwelled more fully in the realm of "being." "Think outside the box" is a wonderful beginning, but only a beginning. Nothing that occurs for you right now is without lessons attached. You seem to learn best through example and so we will continue to create these little vignettes until you catch on and trust what you know. It all comes back to trusting what you know to be true.

You have been given much to contemplate. For now, your contemplation of "limited thought" is your focus for the day and most likely for quite awhile yet to come. Reflecting on this will be an opportunity for you to pay attention to what is limited in the thinking of mankind and in your own daily life. This is yet another opportunity to learn about your human self and how you operate. Look upon these lessons as your chance to expand and to grow into "being." It is simple truth through joyful study.

At the same time you were given this focus, you were told you would not be studying how to heal disease but, rather, how to move beyond the limited thought of disease of the body and more into the act of "being." Though you have practiced for many years to be a healer ministering to mankind's various emotional ailments, it is time to change that view and recognize that even this lofty thought is limited. Healer? Of what do you heal but someone's limited thought? What do you honor when you heal their shortcomings? Bah! Stop it right now. Let me pull you up to the next level of thinking. You do not heal limited thought, and dis-ease is limited thought.

Elevate up the ladder of expanded thought and contemplate "being," and see where that takes you. Quite a different shift of focus isn't it? Do you heal "being"? Well, of course not. Do you think that you stopped working on people, my scribe, healing them as it were, because you were not feeling in alignment? No. You stopped because you remembered somewhere in your true mind that you were harboring a misconception. By addressing their limitations, you were not going one step further or one level beyond limitation into the place of honoring their state of being. You could not do the healing work that addressed only the dis-ease any longer because you no longer existed in that state of untruth yourself. Calm yourself now, for I have pulled the rug of superiority out from under you and it may take you a moment to catch your breath. I can wait.

Now that the ego is shaken up a bit we can again consider *coming forth into being*. This will be a much repeated lesson. We are giving you time to breathe this in. Your resistance is strong today. Your questioning is part of your strength, so do not think I am criticizing you. I honor those quirks in your human self that make you question truth when it literally takes your breath away. The shades are being lifted from your eyes and the truth uncovered. This will set the stage for what is yet to come. Your resistance is always strongest before a greater truth is realized. That is why the message began last night in the shower. These simple truths will reverberate within you for some time before true surrender is achieved. I will be patient.

Remember, I know you and I know that once a truth takes hold the rest that is to come will fly from your fingers onto the keyboard without hesitation. It has been an eventful couple of days, far more than you can possibly imagine. There will be a time when we will sit like this for hours and talk together and learn together. But not now, the work duties of your human life call you to go forth and produce. So go forth, but do so today and every day with the contemplation of "being" in the forefront of your human mind. I am with you always.

*At the end of each morning's message, Mother often left me with a phrase or two of encouragement and contemplation. It was also an acknowledgement of the balancing act I performed each day of touching truth and then delving back into the dream*

*I thought of as my life's reality. I didn't fully understand the importance of that acknowledgment until much later, as the realizations that she shared with me became more and more a part of my daily life and then became for me another lesson to learn and a new truth to experience.*

As we begin to delve into the concept of time travel, as it were, you will see why we have come to you without visual support or auditory confirmation of our existence. Time travel is a lofty subject and one that has oft been interpreted on movie screens and through author imagination until it has taken on an altogether different meaning than was once intended. When I speak of this in the early morning hour, I do so for the express purpose of suspending your belief solely in the here-and-now that you term "your reality," and encouraging you to begin to travel through time without limitation. When we spoke of limitation and freeing the mind from its lofty contemplation of healing disease in another, you were given an example of ego mind at work. Ego mind would like to keep you from delving into unlimited thought patterns and the true nature of your Oneness with God. Time travel, in this instance, simply means your ability to suspend belief in third-dimensional existence long enough to allow you to move more freely within the infinite realities that abound, with each one unto itself a complete thought and actual existence. So the lesson today, acknowledged with great reluctance on your part, is to suspend prejudgment of what is possible and come fly with me through all time and space. How will we do this? Well, take, for example, the time travel that is accomplished when you dream. You lie your body down and suspend, for just a few hours, all distraction. So I say to you, let us walk together in this waking dream and fly into time travel.

Why am I speaking of this now? Your belief that this is impossible for you is perhaps your most difficult judgment to overcome right now. It is my belief that it has to be introduced at this time in order for you to be willing to attempt it in the future. We will do this thing and I believe we will do it rather well. Now, let's get back to the concept of flying, conscious dreaming or time travel, as we have begun to introduce it. This is a lofty thought calling for trust, surrender and action. Do you trust me yet, daughter? Ours is an old memory shared together and you have traveled far through time to this specific universal age to help set the stage once again for change. Let it come. I feel your reluctance, but it needn't be so. We have done this before, traveled at will. We will do so again.

Time travel takes a willingness on your part to suspend disbelief and throw open the doors to all possibility. Do not think too much nor demand too much of yourself at this timing. When it comes upon you, you will know it and become aware of the shift in your reality. We will be subtle—an hour lost or gained, a shift in your location, with perhaps some residual memory of strange happenings. Subtly, we will begin to shift the time travel sequence for you and introduce you once more to all possibility. I have to tell you that this is something you accomplished quite well in the past. However, since you are rearranging your life to accommodate our story, we will ease you into your true reality with great care and honor for the worlds that you balance right now. This is not reluctance on your part, but you are giving us another lesson of the very limited perspective ingrained here and now.

We have much to learn from each other and though you are ever my student, I would not be much of a teacher if I did not acknowledge the gift of learning you give to me each day. You sit in acceptance of a message that hides the messenger from your eyes and ears and the other senses that are the parameters you live within this lifetime. We learn from each other as always, and I am ever humbled by your dedication.

Time travel will enable you to suspend your current reality and move freely outside pervasive belief systems and restrictions. We will use this thought-created mind of yours and put it to a use that is more conducive to the progression of your current journey. In order for us to do this with greater ease, you will practice placing your thoughts on more lofty ideals. So far you have been made aware of your judgments, explored the concept of "coming forth into the act of being" and practiced acceptance and discipline of the mind. Quite a lot has been accomplished in a relatively short period of time.

We have spoken to you of ancient times when we moved easily through the molecules of vibrational frequency and became wholly present in human form. This was quite easily accomplished by the entities that first inhabited—or colonized, if you will—this planet. They materialized within a different environment and began to change it to better suit their needs. Walking through time, through vibrating molecules of multiple existences, was something they did easily because they were, in reality, not completely solidified beings themselves. It is a bit more difficult for humankind now because you have taken on a more solid, or seemingly solid, form. If you attempted this now, you don't believe you would reappear in the same order or arrangement as when you left. I have heard your scientists and those of like minds discussing the concept of transporting themselves by first disassembling their molecules and then reassembling them again in another location. They question how this would be accomplished. What machine could they invent to bring this about? In reality, they have the best machine available to them now, and always have—the unconscious mind. The unconscious mind understands all things physical and spiritual and has the ability to suspend third-dimensional existence and come out of limited thought patterns and into *the act of being*. You and I are going to time travel with ease and at will. You experienced something similar to this when you first began to meditate and were taken on adventures, or, as you called it at the time, your "imaginings." It was all you could acknowledge then, but it was, in truth, your introduction to travel through time and space. You were accessing the unconscious mind while meditating, and these adventures began. They were wonderful adventures, and you will experience them once again in your waking state when the timing is right. For now, subtle changes will be introduced that will begin to expand your awareness of all possibilities. These abilities will become universal and available to all those who are willing to open their minds. Our patience is infinite, and the results will be ongoing. The timing of such events will not be for the purpose of convincing you that these adventures are real. They will simply happen in the course of our work together, but are only one very small portion of it. That is all. Time travel will simply help us to accomplish many things in a timelier manner.

Now you will face the dawn of a new day with a new and, at the same time, ancient memory. I want you to suspend this thought for a moment and visualize that on this morning as the sun rises, you, too, are awakening from a deep sleep of forgetfulness. The symbolism of the rising sun bringing light unto the darkness will assist you to further understand your journey of Self– awareness. Go forth this day and be in joyful awakening.

*The time travel during meditations Mother alluded to were adventurous indeed! While in a meditative state, I would often be taken to beautiful cave-like rooms where I studied with masters of the healing arts, and I used some of their healing techniques on the few people I worked with at that time. I especially remember one occasion where I traveled deep inside the oceans depths off the coast where I live, and was taken inside a dome-shaped structure. On both sides of the long path that ran down the center of this dome were several rooms with arch-like openings. As I walked down this long hall, I could see the colorful, abundant sea life through the bubble-shaped windows scattered throughout the structure. It was an amazing experience. My guide escorted me to a room filled with beings from a former acquaintanceship and lifetime. They seemed very happy to see me and we shared in a celebration that I remember being quite joyful. It was through many such time travels and experiences I began to fully realize the extreme limits we live within on this planet. These travels were both exciting and unreal to me at the same time. Was it my imagination? I truly didn't know. I was surprised when Mother brought the memories of these "travels through time" back to me in this message. It gave me an opportunity to look at these adventures from another perspective, and perhaps that was her purpose all along.*

# CHAPTER THREE

# BELIEF IN THE SELF

It has been seven days since we began this phase of your education, or should I say your "re-education." Seven days of learning together how to trust. We have covered many human emotions in the short time we have been together. Now I have a secret to tell you. We have been together for a very long time this lifetime, a very long time indeed. The how and why of it is not important for what we do now. I simply wanted you to know that our relationship in this lifetime has not been a recent occurrence. We of the collective—that is what we will call ourselves for now—are pleased that you are coming to us with an open heart, an open mind and a discipline that you have always said you lacked. It is time you removed that old shirt and donned a new one. Today we will talk of "belief in the Self" as the touchstone to accomplishing anything you wish but may feel impossible at this time.

A person's belief in the Self begins at a very early age—birth actually. In the process of coming through the birth canal, one has only to experience the trust that must exist between mother and child for the event that will propel this tiny soul from the protection of the warm, nurturing fluid of the womb out into the big, noisy world. And here you arrive, a baby with a mission, and so very, very small that in order to survive at all you must depend on someone else. You have just arrived from a place where your knowledge of divine light and the belief in the Self exists without question. Now you are here, and your belief in the Self will have to be strong in order to survive this period of dependence. You have just discovered how very helpless you are, and so you cry. It is all so limiting and strange, and you wail some more.

Why do I appear to be stating something so obvious? Babies are born, they are dependent and they cry. What you don't realize is they come with a belief in the Self that is woven into the very fiber of their being. They are born knowing and believing they are capable of anything. A baby comes forth with everything it needs, yet is encased in a body that renders it helpless to act upon what it inherently knows to be true. This baby comes forth into the act of being without the ability to *act*, but then that is what growing up is all about. Coming forth into the act of being begins to happen quite soon—the lusty cry, the kicking limbs, the seeking of sustenance that the baby knows it must have in order to survive.

What happens as you grow? Are you nurtured? Do you have comfort in your life? Is someone there to listen and answer your questions? You begin life as a clean slate, and the belief in the Self can grow and develop in loving safety or die from lack of care and attention. Some people can have difficult childhoods yet come through them with a belief in the Self that allows movement forward and a happy life. They grow in loving kindness and seek the God that resides within them. But there are others in similar circumstances that do not move forward or embrace the Self. Those who succeed have a strong memory of their beginning—not in the womb of their earthly mother, but in the arms of God. A baby is born with a strong sense of self that life can challenge right from the start.

"Belief in the Self" is the next phrase after "Come forth into the act of being" and "Believe in the Self." This statement takes you to your next level of enlightenment. Say it often and make it your mantra for the day whenever you forget and become lost in limited thought.

What a beautiful and flawed fairytale it is to accept the beliefs of a teacher who would say, "You can only achieve through me and what I believe. Do not think for yourself. Believe only in me. Trust me to show you what you need, who you are, because I am the way." The Buddha sitting under the tree eating rice, Jesus preaching to the masses —they are products of their personal, unlimited belief in the Self. They did not come to be worshiped, they came to evolve and then to move on. Religions that they did not seek

were built around them. In their lifetimes, they were too busy coming forth
into the act of being, and didn't even consider that what would develop in
their name could lead to wars, death, cruelty and the attempted dominance
of one belief system over the other. So I would caution you now to come
forth into the act of being and to the knowledge that you have always been
whole, capable and loved beyond reason for the God that you are. Perhaps
the Buddha spent so many years under the tree with his eyes closed to shut
out all worldly distractions and get back to that place of all knowing he
possessed in the womb of God. Every moment you allow yourself to come
forth into the act of being, you come closer to the truth of who you are.

So I say "Come forth," for there are those of us who wait to teach you what
you have forgotten to remember and then send you on your way. That is
the key to an enlightened teacher, one who honors what has set them free
and encourages you to go forth and find your own tree to sit under if that is
what you wish to do. Though these great masters are few, they are here and
they will teach you by example, by the spoken word and in any way that
you can be reached. Step out of your self-imposed womb-like existence
and take those first toddling steps. If you fall down, get up and try it again
until strength of character is achieved, the strength in the belief of the Self
into the act of being that has always been with you. Come forth into the
act of being and believe in the Self once again. Nurture one another and
laugh often for the sheer joy of the experience. With smiles and laughter
in abundance I leave you as the sun comes up and your day begins. Until
we meet again, I am the hand that gently guides you on your way.

*During the first few weeks—months, actually—I continued to have some days when
I simply couldn't wrap my mind around the material I was transcribing. I didn't
feel smart or clever enough to truly comprehend what she was saying. I wondered if
I was transcribing correctly, interfering with the message in any way or missing the
point entirely. During these times I would usually create some sort of a distraction
to interrupt the dictation. Mother always took the time to get me back on track in a
way I couldn't discount.*

*I have always listened to her messages and transcribed them on the computer with
my eyes closed. This helps me to concentrate and not become overly concerned with*

*my numerous spelling errors and the missed key strokes made in the rush to get her words on the page. On this particular morning, I took a peek at my transcription after the first paragraph and noticed that one statement you will soon see was all in capital letters! Now, I know I didn't do this accidentally, given the lower case type that appears on either side of that sentence. But the message for me was crystal clear. She was raising her voice a bit to make her point. I got it. Enough said.*

Begin your day with a mantra, a chant that is spoken internally for you alone. I HAVE GIVEN YOU SOMETHING TO CONTEMPLATE, TO COME FORTH INTO THE ACT OF BEING, TO BELIEVE IN THE SELF…AND I HAVE NOT FOUND YOU WANTING IN THAT REGARD. This is, in truth, the light that will guide you when you go through the many levels I have mentioned before. I want you to know that you are moving through these levels quite rapidly. You are beginning to remember to trust completely, and we will count on that trust to always be present when we are together. This is still practice time, though you may feel you have practiced enough.

Remember when we traveled to the caves of healing during some of your early meditations and you wrote down what you saw and the experiences you had? Do you remember? We will visit once more these cave-like rooms of learning, but you will do so in the person of human form. Now, how will that be possible? Well, I will tell you this: you will not be sitting on this chair typing on these keys when we do it. The time for scribing and the time for moving about are separate. If you wish, you will write it down afterwards and add the experiences to typed pages, but for now we sit and get the rhythm of each other. It is at times more difficult than we first thought, but still easily accomplished.

Now let me tell you a story of when we made a brief visit to the caves located near the area now known as the Himalayas. Buried deep within was a cavern of many rooms. These rooms had been there since the beginning of the creation of these mountains. They were inhabited by those who had come forth to set up a place of contemplation, healing and regeneration for the individuals coming from beyond this universe—some from the Pleiades and some from far beyond even that. The rooms were lit from within and quite comfortable. Why did they dwell first in these caves? The world outside was going through upheaval and new birth. Inside and sheltered within these rooms, we were safe from flying rock, molten lava and the storms that raged. Your planet was, in some respects and in some locations, still being formed. There were those who were living on the surface, creating, planning and shaping life on this new planet, and they were, at times, in need of respite. These caves were much like a way station for those early explorers, who would go out onto the burgeoning earth and toil upon it and then come back to rest and heal. I guess you could say these caves were rather like the earth's first "spa" experience. They remain to this day, but in another dimension that cannot be seen by humankind at this time. We came to these caves because it was what we wished to do. We were not teacher and student then, you and I, simply beings who were on a new adventure together. Mankind has need of these caves and their wonderful healing properties now more than ever.

You watch the news on your TV and hear the scientists talk of global warming and the melting ice caps and you ponder the fate of this little planet. I will tell you this: nothing lasts forever, not even your beautiful earth. Take heart, you will not be leaving en masse to colonize another universe. Not yet anyway, and definitely not with a rocket ship as your vehicle. This planet is going through its own evolution of spirit and waking up into the act of being, much as you, mankind, are changing and becoming the receptacle for new and evolutionary experiences. This will bring about many climate changes. These shifts in consciousness have actually been occurring throughout the world for quite some time. It is not time to panic, for you have seen many missives written about the end of the world before—even a quite interesting story in the Bible called Revelation, I believe. Evolution and upheaval of some sort has always been part of the universal cycle, and your planet is forever changing. Mankind can learn a lot by observing what has begun on this planet. The changes that are now reported in your news media are accurate. The polar ice is melting and the climate is changing. Some species are dying, while others are being discovered for the first time—hairy lobsters, and even birds and monkeys never seen before. The evolution of the planet and the human consciousness has arrived. Some scientists are aware of the climate changes and keep reminding the public at large that this has always been a volatile planet and change is expected. If you wanted a nice, calm and peaceful place to live, you should have gone to the moon. Instead, here you are on a planet that is really quite an extraordinary place to be, quite extraordinary indeed. Recorded history does not even begin to describe what has occurred here from the true beginning. But we will keep that information for another time.

Now back to the caves. We joined the group already within the caves and placed upon the walls and entrances the raised lettering that told all who entered that this was a place of healing. We were scribes even then, you and I. We set up shop and began the business of comforting and repairing those who came back from work on the surface. The colonization of this newly forming world was exciting and filled with adventure. We were in the process of creating and were much like the artist who paints on a canvas, takes a step back to view his creation and then comes forth again to rub something out, refine and paint it over to create anew. We will go once again to these caves, you and I, because I want you to remember what was accomplished there and bring the essence of it forth once more. These caves will become available to those who want to experience the future elevation of this planet. There is still much for you to learn and experience, and a great need to reawaken the ancient wisdom that will help to bring this planet through any turmoil and strife that may come. Don't go home and start packing away food stuffs and building your own cellars. Your evolution will depend on your willingness to open to new ways of thinking and of being. This time we bring forth truth through many who will scribe it and live it and teach it to others. It may be a small group of adventurers at first. It was before, and look what they accomplished taking one step at a time. We are following an ancient script and adding the pages as we go.

Long ago we stood together, you and I, coming from another universe and dimensional existence and contemplating what could be accomplished on this emerging, volatile planet. How could we best shape this new land of volcanoes and earthly tremors? In actuality, we were not the first to set foot upon this land. There were others before us who had come from a far greater distance. They stopped to explore for a bit and then simply moved on. They are known as "travelers," a people who live only to explore but never colonize or inhabit other lands. These travelers search out new territories then recorded their findings. They are of a single mind and purpose, and those of us who had come here learned much from their shared experience. We lived in these deep underground caves in a cocoon of safety as part of a collective who populated and worked on this emerging planet, bringing knowledge of other places and times. It was quite an enjoyable beehive of activity and camaraderie and an exciting time to watch the earth grow and become one of the most delightful planets in the galaxies. There were rooms that held underground rivers with an endless supply of water needed to sustain life and to grow a variety of plants within the caves. Some of us could create whatever we wished instantly by projecting our thought patterns outward. But in the spirit of new adventure, we wanted to also experience growing something from seed to maturation. I have to tell you, it felt very good. It wasn't something that we had done for some time and the experience of watching something develop from a little seed into a thriving plant was exhilarating. However, in the true spirit of experimentation, we would often accelerate the growth process to see what would happen. It was soon apparent that some things take time to develop and mature, and an opportunity to contemplate a new way of thinking was presented.

Why am I going on about growing plants? It will help explain how we came to view and to assist mankind in populating the planet. Much as we watched the seeded plant grow into maturation, we also observed humankind evolve into being. Remember "come forth into the act of being"? This was the beginning time for those beings that first inhabited the earth, and they were much like the seeds planted on this newly forming planet; these new human seedlings came from many diverse universes. We fussed around a bit until human evolution on this planet took off and could maintain itself without outside interference. Now when I caution you to "come forth into the act of being," you know that it is also to bring forth the memories of these ancient times. Your continued evolution depends on how well you remember to come forth into the act of being. The second part of that phrase—"and believe in the Self"—will bring you home. This "home" has its origins in the beginning of time.

When we came to your world, we came with no disease of the body, no warring factions, no pain, no sorrow, no limit or excitement. Yes, I said "excitement." No thrill of adventure. We were highly evolved and no one ever starved or was homeless, lame or angry in our world. We were very advanced indeed and as good as dead. It was at this exact time in our evolution that we decided we had missed something in our development, and so we went adventuring to find it. We have learned a great deal from watching you grow, and you continually surprise us in the variety of ways in which you choose to live your lives. Throughout history, there were times when you came close to destroying your world and some of us stepped in to prevent it. But other than that, we have interfered very little. Why do we come to speak to you now? That is a good question and I don't know if I can give you a complete answer as yet. I only know that we observe the sorrow and see the dying and want to bring you back to life. We watch in awe at what you have accomplished and can't help but take note of how much you have forgotten of your origin. I do not want you to think of your present existence as if you were lab rats in someone else's grand scheme, possessing little voice to future outcome. Not true. You have free will now, but there was a time you didn't have it. Some of you were initially planted much as the seed of a plant and you had to be nurtured and tended in order to grow and develop minds of your own. It was a time of great learning and you taught us much in the process. Now you have free will and have been allowed to go about the business of your own success and failure. You have learned that free will always carries a price. That price is a responsibility to yourself and to the world you inhabit. One of the reasons we are here now is that you have called us to assist in the evolution of your planet. In actuality, we have always been here and remained in close contact with some of you. But for others, by prior agreement before they came, we have had to reach down and shake them up a bit to get their attention once more. Now is the time to move forward in earnest, for a new and expanded world is upon you. That is why we are here and are spreading the messages to so many at the same time.

It is time for you to wake unto the early morning hours when the electrical current and the interfering sound and vibrations of human existence are quieted. Early morning is the time you can be free of all distraction and breathe with focus and listen. It is time once again to come forth into the act of being and believe, *really believe*, in the Self. Believe in what you *know* to be true. Your brain has lain dormant for a long time and will be awakened in those who are willing. New ways of being, thinking and living are upon you. Not all will share this adventure, but some will, and that is where we begin. Why do we come now? Because it is time to weed the garden called "mankind." You, every one of you, have called it forth. It is not something we have decided. We are not your God, but we do retain the knowledge of the truth of our origin, and that truth lives within every one of you yet forgotten. Why have we come now? We have come to awaken those memories. It is time to grow mankind, to evolve in earnest, and take those emotions of love, thanksgiving and reverence for all things and make them into a beautiful garden called "your world." Your planet is changing, evolving, dying the old and creating the new. As the inhabiting humans of this world, you are changing also. It is why we came —to lend a hand. Listen to the scribes and oracles who speak truth. Be cautious of those who would tell you they are the way, for this is not what we speak. Listen with your heart to the truth of who you are. And come forth into the act of being and believe in the Self. There are no false gods before you, only the false promises made by mortals. Know the difference.

CHAPTER FOUR

# THOUGHT PROJECTION

"Come forth into the act of being and believe in the Self" has many layers that can be analyzed and discussed word by word if desired, but for now, the most important phrase within this declaration is "into the act of being," which requires a deeper commitment—one of time and thought, of stated purpose and discussion; a deeper commitment to contemplation and questioning until another part of the mantra is revealed, the one that will assist you to continue and to truly believe in the Self. Your current assignment is the contemplation of "being" and the discovery of your many thoughts and judgments, especially those not realized until now. This will be an ongoing process throughout your lifetime. Begin your deliberation without fear and view it as a new adventure and a new frontier to explore. You will soon come to realize that it really isn't new to you at all but is yet another level of understanding made possible by your willingness to explore.

Now, let me take you once again into the caves when your planet first began. Many wonders were being created every day through thought projection. And in the process, we discovered a way in which to view these thoughts prior to manifesting them. When we first began to manifest our thought projections, the outcome and the possible effect these manifestations might have on someone else or the earth as a whole were not foremost in our mind. As a result, we learned to first project a thought onto a screen for viewing. In this way we were able to perfect the action of thought and, thus, control the result. Many potential problems were discovered and averted during this process that could have had devastating results if allowed to manifest.

We marvel at how completely unrestrained and easily manipulated many of your thought patterns have come to be. Some of mankind's collective thought projections have been disastrous and caused unnecessary upheaval in the world and most certainly climate changes on a global level, from lack of awareness of the power of your thoughts. Living in a constant state of fear, for example, influences and perpetuates disasters. At a later time, we will begin teaching you the way to view your thought patterns and then you can begin to edit and refine the outcomes for yourself.

While residing in the caves, we continued to develop and further refine our thought projections and discovered many of them had been influenced and shaped by the remote thoughts of others. It had always been common practice to occasionally join our thoughts together with others of like mind in order to create and achieve a common result through group effort. Our work in the caves was one example of this type of cooperation. Initially, we assumed we had complete mastery of our individual thought patterns, as well as those thoughts formed cooperatively for the common good of all. We were greatly disturbed to discover that secondary thoughts outside our control could have and were having an influence on the outcome. This was a vastly important revelation to us, as we considered ourselves superior throughout the universe in our ability to create through projected thought. We were humbled by this discovery and very eager to learn from the experience. What we learned will assist you in avoiding a similar circumstance as you learn to refine your own thought projections.

It is now time for you to seriously consider the absolute power of individual and collaborative thought projections, and I am speaking to you as a fellow creator. You will be pleased to know that it is already a very refined ability in all of you. Look at what you have created in your life and the world around you, and you will begin to understand why I took you back into the caves of learning where we first began on your planet so you might fully awaken and take responsibility for your actions. You have been projecting thoughts and creating what you will for millions of years. Your thoughts have been joined with the thoughts of others and as a result, societies and cultures have been formed, wars have been fought, and fear and hate perpetuated. But at the same time you have also created great peace and infinite beauty. And as with any skill that one possesses, it can be used for purposeful good or with harmful intent. You have done both. Perhaps it is time now to contemplate and refine through your personal thought projections what it is you wish to create and experience in your life and the world as a whole, and do so from this time forward.

There have been many teachers over the years that have come to tell you your purpose and have shared certain techniques to improve your life. They have told you, "As you think, so you are" and given you many insights to consider. I have taken you back to the very beginning of your planet, deep within the caves of learning where it all began, to empty your mind of all preconceived notions, distractions and erroneous beliefs clouding your mind. Sweep them all away. Now you are ready to come forth into the act of being. You will *act* upon this clean slate as if you were the most brilliant and learned gods, for you are truly that and much more. You will *act* as if there is nothing in the way of your ability to accomplish all that you desire. You will have total confidence and complete belief in the Self. You are standing on the planet Earth and you are ready. It is time for you to put into practice the mantra you have been given. The seed has been planted so you may write upon your clean slate and create your day, your year and the rest of your life with greater awareness. How will you proceed? Do not be afraid. You are not alone. There are many who have come to assist mankind in this new adventure. It is truly an exciting time.

So let's start with something big, shall we? I say we create the sun rising in the morning sky, and if there are clouds, I say we project rain. You think this is cheating? Not so. You are using past memories of projected events, and this is allowed. You can use these memories to your advantage. Project a thought, *the rain will come.* All right then, where is the rain? Is instant gratification necessary for you to continue to focus your thought in this direction? Just because your thoughts may not produce results immediately doesn't mean they are any less potent. There are often circumstances that surround your manifestations that need to be aligned before results can be realized, and being mindful of the ramifications of any thought projection beforehand is very important.

From a focus of intense anger, one might project a thought that corresponds to this emotional state and produce harmful results when least expected. This can be dangerous if one has been manipulated into certain belief patterns. The Jewish Holocaust during World War II is just such an example. Throughout history, those of the Jewish faith have often lived with persecution of one kind or another. During World War II, resentment and fear of the Jewish population was projected into the minds of the populace, and group thoughts were joined together with preconceived beliefs and judgments. The projected thoughts of just such beliefs, when focused together by scores of humans, have produced some horrifying results throughout the ages. To this day, persecution continues in many parts of the world, and mankind needs to be aware of the consciousness of group thought patterns that continue to produce harmful results. You have been given this example to illustrate what projected thought can create when manipulated by prejudice and joined together in focused thought. But projected thought can also create great beauty and kindness, love and caring, and rescue disaster victims from death or release a loved one to journey in peace. The intent of your thoughts is always pivotal to any creation. Your thought projections don't limit your life, they create it. At times you may let your thoughts be controlled and focused by others, so you project thought collectively and create accordingly—for example, a call for world peace or a cure for polio. But when you do not pay attention to your personal thought projections, the results can be devastating. Always endeavor to look honestly and with total awareness to what it is you intend, and practice viewing your projected thoughts on a screen of your own making.

For now we ask only that you consider what has been presented. Allow your increased awareness and insight to help you view your screen clearly and remove any harmful and manipulated thought forms from your projections. Be aware when you have joined your thoughts with others and been manipulated by outside influence. Also look at the times you broke away from the group consciousness and created something beautiful. Do this on an individual basis and you will begin to see the power that comes from taking ownership of your thoughts and allowing yourself to come forth into the act of Being. The veil is beginning to lift, and perhaps you begin to see creation in a different light. The process of your enlightened awareness will be ongoing. Each person on this planet has a solitary journey in which to learn how thought projection influences your life, the life of others and the planet as a whole, and to learn from it as we did.

When we first decided to examine our projected thought patterns and see exactly what we were doing, we learned more than we could have imagined. The same thing is happening now to the inhabitants of planet earth in very subtle ways. We talked before about certain sayings such as "thinking outside the box" and how they open the mind to an array of possibilities. So, let's now begin to dissect your thought projections and see what we come up with. First, erase the screen of the mind, the ego or whatever one calls it today, and relax. This is not a time for punishment or judgment, just introspection and the thrill of learning something new. Clearing the mind is more difficult than expected, isn't it? But you can do it. Sweep it clean. Focus only on the here and now and the information you have been given. Practice sweeping clean all your thought projections and any other influences—and there are many that might be lurking in the shadows. Beautiful, isn't it, to just take this moment to *be*? No memories. No agendas for the day. No hopes. No fears. No expectations.

Can you ever have a completely blank screen? No, not really, for the part of your essence that inhabits this body comes from All That Is and is contained within this limited vehicle called "human." In the process of this containment, the human projects what it believes itself to be as influenced by cellular memory and packs this into the structure called "human." The mind or slate is then filled instantly with thought projections from past attitudes and values. When one dies, then All That Is releases the body, and the Soul remembers and retains the truth. Completely clearing the mind while still encased in the human body is a little tricky, but it can be done.

Many of you have been taught that cellular memory, karma and recurring lifetimes (called reincarnation) are for the purpose of working on what you have not yet completed and perfecting your Soul essence. By holding onto a belief such as this, you are perpetuating limited thought. I am asking you instead to create thoughts that are *unlimited*. Let's get back to the clean slate which you can project as cleansed with only a thought. Try it and see. I'll wait. Good. Now, what do you say we start with today and with you? One thought only. It can be anything—one single, unlimited, purely unique thought. Now take this projected thought and look at it. Make it your own creation without judgment. You don't want any interference or prejudice to impede this one, wholly unique created thought. Look at it projected on your screen and say, "Well done." There are no limits here, no harm to anyone and no karma attached. No cellular memory to muddy the waters, just pure, individual projected thought. Now that went so well, so let's try another. Place your thought there beside the first one on your screen and project away. Use the same parameters—unlimited and without interference. Now you are beginning to see what can happen when you become conscious of your thought patterns and learn to take control of the events in your life. It is during this lifetime that I want you to make the journey back to Original Thought and discover the absolute knowing of who you are and who you have created yourself to be this time around. For now, concentrate on taking one step at a time and I promise that opportunities will open up for you that you had no idea were even possible. Practice your thought projections, clean the slate and do it again. See what you can create from such conscious awareness. Some things will be instantaneous; others will take longer to develop and to bring to fruition. Right now you are practicing and learning to clean your slate, project thought and become unlimited in your act of *being*. This is a wonderful beginning, is it not?

So, now let us speak once more of healing, since we touched briefly on this subject before. I will bring you back again to the caves where we first brought specific methods of healing from other worlds and other vibrational dimensions. When first we came to the caves from beyond this universe, we brought with us the knowledge and expectation of continued good health of the body. When symptoms of an illness or dis-ease began to manifest, we immediately examined any projected thoughts that had created the problems, began the healing process by forming new thought patterns and quickly manifested renewed health. Dis-ease didn't happen too often in the mature adults of our kind but occasionally occurred in the young, who were still learning to refine their thoughts.

Many years ago, my scribe was introduced to how projected thought relates to curing physical disease. She was part of a group of like-minded individuals asked to focus their collective thoughts on complete health for a woman who was going in for surgery, then project these thoughts together for her rapid recovery. This is a good and positive focus to practice at any time. It was during this specific meditation that I directed her to focus through the mind's eye and visually scan this woman's body while moving her hands in a sweeping motion from head to toe and front to back. As a result, she noticed several darkened areas adjacent to the spine and across the area of her lungs that had not yet been diagnosed by medical doctors. It was a warning of future dis-ease and was a method of diagnosis and healing taught to my scribe during previous lifetimes. The darkened spots in her body were not yet manifested areas of illness at the time but were the imprint of projected thought patterns with the potential to create cancer, or the body turning back upon itself. With the women's permission, given on a soul level, my scribe began erasing this future dis-ease and helped to do away with her problem before it became manifest. This was accomplished through her remembered ability to project thought and the single focus to heal and eliminate any dis-ease of the body.

What is the patient's role in all of this? Before healing can take place, permission must be obtained from the person to be healed. Without this permission, nothing you do can ever bring forth the desired result. It is this collaboration between two souls with a single purpose that enables one to heal. We very seldom had to obtain this cooperation in the caves because we were of like mind and knew our individual roles in the healing process. It was at a much later time in the earth's evolution that this spirit of cooperation had to be reignited for those upon your planet who had forgotten to remember. When focused on healing, it is important to remember that not everyone can or will agree to be healed. A healer must let go of the outcome. The agreement you make with the soul of another is not to project what you want or desire but to allow what *they* want and desire and then present them with alternatives to dis-easement. What decisions they make are their own. You can only provide the opportunity for them to live without disease, if that is their choice. For some, the disease is what they desire. But for you, mankind, the focus is to come forth into the act of Being. In the beginning, as my student, my scribe would see these same lessons applied wherever we traveled. She learned not to judge but only provide the tools to transport the embodiment out of such discomfort, if so desired. Healing dis-ease of any kind is a serious responsibility. *For the most part, illness is caused by those who have forgotten to daily project the focus of perfect health on a clean slate.* It is like a morning ablution, one we had been taught from an early age. We used this technique for any occasion in our daily life. This is a technique you would do well to practice. Start small with one projected thought: perfect health. Focus daily on that and see what comes of it.

Our focus upon this planet will always be to come forth into the act of being. What we will continue to teach is how to apply this mantra in your daily life. You have had lesson one, projecting good health upon your screen. This is where the healing, true healing, begins to happen. We will start from there. Scan your body, feel the areas of dis-easement or the areas that feel out of alignment and project good health and balance onto those areas. Use the tools that you have brought with you for this purpose, the tools of your inner vision, and your *belief in Self*. Use these tools and the rest will follow. Start there. Start now. You have your assignment.

I ask that you hold this day and every day in reverence. Greet each dawn that heralds enlightenment upon the earth. It is a new beginning that is, in fact, very old. Always remember that you possess special gifts brought forth from many universal dimensions. Though much of mankind has forgotten, each of you will begin this remembering in your own little corner of the world and illume the space where you live. Many bright lights will be shining with similar teachings, as the remembering moves out to fill the world. The universe will begin to radiate beautiful light as your knowledge and acceptance of Original Thought increases. We have come forth, those of us from the past—which is really not the past at all—to help return you to what you have always known. You have taught us much and we are grateful, so we repay you in kind by helping to ease the limits of this dimension and bring you more into balance with the universal order. Come forth into the act of being and believe in the Self, and then you will know.

# CHAPTER FIVE

# JUDGMENT AND THE ACT OF BEING

Listen mankind and remember that all things are possible with a simple mind. *All things.* A mind free of distraction or complication is almost impossible here on terra, but it can be done. My scribe and I have come each day in the early morning hours before dawn to eliminate the distractions of the day, though some continue to persist. Mankind, you will soon learn how to live on this planet without distraction, and the first step will be to *let go of judgment.*

I spoke to my scribe one evening during a time when her mind was quiet, to spark these knowings and conscious thought patterns so they could be brought forth when we sat together for transcribing. I told her that judgment is not totally exclusive to humankind, but that judgment, in one form or another, exists in all realms. Judgment was inherent from the beginning, and to some spiritualists this may sound almost heretical. Even so, it is the truth. We judge. We make choices based on judgment every day. Most of our judgments are superficial, but many are deeply ingrained in the unconscious mind of Original Thought.

How can Original Thought be judgmental? Original Thought came forth and placed a universal order upon the heavens, the stars, the planets, human form and everything that was to be. It was the beginning. Original Thought gazed out at what had been created, and there was judgment and a bit of tweaking as to what would continue to evolve and what would not. Judgment existed as part of Original Thought's creation. Even your legendary Jesus judged and would find wanting in the many things He experienced. It is also true that He possessed the capacity for great love and devotion, but still He judged. Why this lecture on judgment? It is because I want you to accept judgment as part of the whole of creation and then move beyond it. When you refuse to accept truth as presented, you stop your forward motion. Make judgment work for you and for the betterment of mankind. Do not dwell in righteousness by assuming you are without judgment and, therefore, superior to those who are obviously not as enlightened as you. This is simply not true, and we are ever the purveyors of truth. We judge. We have judged from the beginning and we will always judge. It is part of who we are and part of our inheritance from Original Thought.

From Original Thought—God, if you will—the creation of all things was brought forth upon the vastness of space. What was created was moved around a bit, shifted, compressed, rejected or refined then allowed to evolve further, and subsequently become what you see today. This was all accomplished with a little dash of judgment along the way. This judgment helped to weigh in the balance what would continue and what would be discontinued and removed. The beginning of Original Thought creation upon this barren landscape was very volatile and kinetic. Sparks were flying, the heavens were rolling, the sound deafening. Could there be sound without anyone to hear? Of course, Original Thought was there. In the vastness were colors, sights and sounds and a cacophony of turbulence. And running through it all was the thread of judgment, the picking and choosing of what goes and what stays. Do not tell me you are without judgment when, in the face of Original Thought, you see it present from the beginning. This is, in reality, a judgment in and of itself, is it not? Some of you have learned that to judge is wrong but to allow all things is righteous. Now, if that isn't a judgment, I don't know what is! When one says he or she is without judgment and accepting of all things, be wary. This little sojourn into the existence of judgment will serve you well in the days to come.

I have told my scribe that our coming together in such a way as this will be judged by some. But by then she will have moved beyond the need to defend anything that is written, accepted judgment and continued her forward momentum. Judgment will not have as great an effect on her as in the past. She did not expect the story about Original Thought's judgment and had a great deal of prejudice about recording something that was the opposite of what she had accepted as truth and learned from many great Masters. Yet she still came to me every morning before the dawn and brought her judgments, for they are as much a part of her as her breath. She is strong- willed and determined, dogmatic in her pursuit of truth, and I would have her no other way.

So, bring your judgment along and shake the cobwebs from your opening mind. But hang on, mankind for there is more to come. We are going to shake you up a bit. You will receive information every now and then that you don't agree with. This information will help to clarify what has already been given, as well as prepare you for what is to come. I have judged you worthy, mankind. This is an auspicious time and a very important next step that has permitted a shift in your consciousness.

The world is not your concern—the death, the dying, pollution and war. The diseases of the body are not your concern. I could go on and on, for there is truly no end to the laments of the earth bound human. What has been created or what has been lost can never be regained, nor can the footsteps be retraced in the search for what might have been. You learn and you go on. It is that simple. You may wish to examine every flaw of your character, their character, this choice, that choice ad infinitum, but for what purpose? *What you have created in your personal life and what has been created by any human living here now is simply your creation.* The ramifications of these life choices echo and vibrate today within your Soul. Should I tell you to be concerned about all of this and to lament your lot in life—the bad parenting, the abusive husband, the "devil made you do it"? I think not. To belabor these experiences is wasting time.

Now that I have your attention and you are through judging what I have just stated, I will explain. I want you to understand that *caring* and *having concern* are two separate things, quite separate in intention and outcome. To *care* about an event, a person or an outcome is to take it on as your own. Must you actually be in Africa to stop the genocide of the people there? No. But you must *own* the genocide. By owning it, you absorb the hatred, the death and the quiet pain of those individuals who do not know what you know. How can you do this and stay sane? That is a very good question. What if I were to tell you that you already do it and you are quite sane? What do you think of that? To care and to own the suffering, to own the wars, to own the homeless that you walk by on the street, is to accept first and then rise above this acceptance and see beyond it.

How can you *care* and not be *concerned*? I want you to practice something with me. I want you to focus on that homeless man asleep on the street with the dirty clothes and alcohol- drenched cells. Really *see* him, and then picture him as a baby, brand new and ready to be shaped and formed in this lifetime by the many people and events yet to come. Hold this baby in your thoughts with everything that you are right now and everything that you know, and focus on this tiny, clean slate. What do you see? Is it innocence? Hope? Destiny? Yes. You see all this, and even more that cannot be known until it is. Hold this baby in your arms. How can you really *care* without touching in some way the human? You don't want to touch the grown man with alcoholic breath and dirty clothes who sleeps on the street. Better to hold the baby in your arms with the clean smell and wrapped in a soft blanket. You hold this baby and you see everything that he will go through in life. You see all the happiness, the pain, the sorrow, the travails, the injuries, the losses and the gains, and you hold him close to your heart. And you *care* enough to allow him everything.

Can you change the eventual outcome for him? Perhaps, for you have held him and felt his heart beating against yours. But you have also cared enough to lay him down gently so his life may be allowed to continue as it will. What more can you do? Will you feel the same compassion for him when you again walk by his sleeping form on the street? Maybe you will remember holding him as that newborn, or simply forget and quickly walk away. But you most certainly will not stop and pick him up. Your concern and any pain you may feel for him might not extend to touching him in the adult form. I hear your thoughts and the judgment of your actions. How could you be so uncaring? Where is your concern for the betterment of all mankind? I hear you and have also seen you walk by the homeless on the street without as much as a glance in their direction. What I am seeking for you to know is that true caring comes from your ability to see the homeless man as he was as a baby and to focus your caring there.

Is it too radical and confusing an idea for who you perceive yourself to be now? Concerned, you may give money to organizations, attend rallies, march in parades and pray to change one event, one human, one thought or state of being. You desire change to happen by showing your concern through action. This is not a problem. It does not hurt anything and may even help. Expressing concern for your planet, your fellow man and events that take place in the world is never a bad thing. But I am asking you to step out of the box of limitation once again and look at another way in which to show concern. I am asking you to take it to yet another level called "caring," for yourself and for your fellow man as well. *Until you step out of the box of supposed outcome, and begin to nurture and care for who you are as the Self, nothing will change.* It is what we are asking of the collective you at this time. It may appear selfish to speak of caring about yourself when you see a world that seems to be focused so completely on its own self-interest. Truly, it is not self-interest that motivates man, but rather the lack of understanding of who he really is in truth.

When we first came to journey in the caves of learning and to envision on our screen what our projected thoughts were creating, we found a need to take a step back before time existed, to the place of Original Thought, and then move forward from there once again. It was a radical idea but the only way in which we were truly able to proceed successfully. We needed to remember our source, Original Thought, and we had to come forth into being that thought, that focus, once again. We did all this from a place of caring, not from concern but from caring for the Self as an integral part of Original Thought. We gained greater wisdom in the process.

You see the wars, the genocide, the death, the quaking of the earth and the poverty, and you are *concerned*. You forget that you are viewing the people and the events brought about by lack of memory of one's origin. When you are caring and believe in the Self, then your journey will assist that homeless man to rise from the street and begin his own passage back to the Self realized and to the healing that makes all things possible. It can be done, but it will take great willingness on the part of the few who take that solitary journey back to Original Thought and are then able to come forth into the act of being and believe in the Self. The evolution of caring and the change in any condition must first come from the Self. All the answers are within each of you, and the discovery of these answers is the journey and the path that we travel.

We are about the true understanding of the Self on the journey of *caring*. Throughout this planet there are many Souls with similar pursuits, some as solitary individuals or in community with others. Each one has the courage to venture back to caring, back to Original Thought, and are then willing to come forth. It is the only way in which change can take place. You will never be alone in this process. Do not be concerned when some say you need to suffer in order to gain enlightenment because that belief is ridiculous. You do not have to suffer. What would be the point?

I have held out my hand to you and you have willingly placed yours within it. Though my grasp is strong, I am not pulling you forward but walking beside you instead, for I care about you and your journey and have walked this path before, as have you many, many times. The homeless man upon the street can learn from our experience and begin his own journey. Do you think there is no one standing beside him as he sleeps? We are there. We are everywhere, waiting for you to awaken, always patiently waiting.

As you change how you live your life by caring enough to take this solitary path, then the man on the street wakes a little more, the wars stop for moments of time, the hatred and the killing and the hopeless poverty pauses but a breath—just from your decision to make this journey. Think how very powerful your caring about the Self can be in just this one pivotal moment of choice! How powerful would it be if thousands or millions or even billions of individuals made that commitment to journey back to Original Thought and to the simplicity of coming forth into the act of being? This is truly the heaven of which the Bible speaks.

Sadly, over time, the Bible's teaching have often become a means to control rather than to express the caring that I am asking of you right now. Do it anyway, and you will be gently guided along the way. Start from this one point in time, in this slice of your reality called "human," and care about yourself enough to change it all forever. It starts with you and a single purpose.

There may be people who will accuse you of being selfish when, in fact, you are being truly self-less for perhaps the first time. You have no idea how powerful the result will be when you begin to care for your own journey back to Original Thought and then are willing to come forth into the act of being. It is a great act of courage on your part, and the only way to make the most of this journey and to move forward; truly the only way. It is enough for now, for this seed has been planted.

I am truly amazed at the beauty as well as the pain that I observe here, for I remember when first we began to venture forth from the caves and onto this planet. Now mankind has been on the surface experiencing life for a very long time, but without the ability to rest and heal as we did in the caves. You have been on your own for millions of years without respite. A few of you have opened enough to journey beyond this limited existence through meditation and devotion to an ideal, but not many and not for long. There are also those of you who have committed to bringing mankind back into the womb of the Mother and to the healing and peace that was found in the caves. Come with me and journey forth, caring for the Self and then back to Original Thought and to another adventure waiting beyond even that. It is a journey worth taking. Think upon it today. Be kind to yourself in the process. Be gentle to the one who is just emerging from the womb of Mother. Be loving and thoughtful to your Self today. By doing so, you will not only survive, you will *thrive*.

# CHAPTER SIX

# THE SPARKS FROM ORIGINAL THOUGHT

Let us travel back into the void…back before Original Thought was formed. Back before the darkness delivered the dawn of time and filled the space with the rhythm and sound of humanity without end. Back into the spaces between the birth of it all. Journey back until it swallows you whole and tosses you out to reassemble the void. Then visit the silence. Breathe it in, and all the spaces in between. Allow yourself to simply be in the moment. Though it is difficult to duplicate here in totality, when we wake our scribe in the early morning hour we give her the essence of this silence so she may begin to remember the void and her beginning. Swimming in this embryonic fluid of creative force, Original Thought emerged from this emptiness and birthed itself into the universal order.

The caves in the Himalayas were the womb for the birth of humanity upon your planet, and the true birthplace of your emerging thought patterns. In the quiet morning hours, I asked my scribe if she remembered when she first experienced the idea of Original Thought in her dream state. The swirling mass of electric sparks danced to creation's tune while she watched her birth into being. She placed this dream on her projected screen and remembered, much as we had been motivated to do in the caves of learning. There was a time in the caves when we traveled back into the realm of Original Thought and observed where we had drifted away from the impeccability of our own thought projections. During this process, as in her dream state, we saw this same spinning vortex swirling and pulsating in the void, forming a spiral that expanded, twirled and danced across the darkness, while the inner core moved out to touch the boundaries of time and space yet to be created. Sparks ignited and began to separate from this spinning vortex to become the sparks of existence. The sun was formed and the planets grew as your universe became whole in this swirling dance of light.

Your planet was visited by those of us from a far, distant universe. We were also the children of Original Thought, and from our beginning we went out into the void to grow and to explore, to taste and touch and create. We were given form, we created form and we played in this swirling universal matter of creation. We had strong memories of this beginning, and when we arrived on your planet we were able to create and experiment quite easily. But in the course of our creative development, we found it necessary to go back to Original Thought's origin to learn where we had made a wrong turn in our projected thought patterns. We went back and touched the purest of time. We went back to the creation of Original Thought, and we remembered. It was there where we breathed in the void, lived the expansion that filled the space and experienced our conception once again. And it is through this alignment with Original Thought that you will be able to come forward into the act of being with grace and certainty. Be glad for this opportunity to stretch your wings and fly unheeded into each new day with renewed purpose and spirit. This alignment with Original Thought's purpose places you literally back at the beginning of time and clarifies the intention of the act of being.

The purpose of this alignment is twofold: It is always good to be aware, first, from whence you came and, second, where you are going. I ask you now to consider in what direction you wish to travel. How will you get there and what will you do when you arrive? By now I hope you know the direction that we have committed to travel. It is our intent to awaken known truths, as well as explore new ideas for further study and reflection. Through your understanding of projected thought, Original Thought and your individual purpose, you will bring these truths into the open once more and come forth into the act of being and believe in the Self. You are in the process of cleaning the slate of misguided thought and beliefs, letting go of what does not serve you and learning to create at will from truth. You will learn how to do this completely and without hesitation.

I have given you a very brief introduction to the course of action for what we do and what we will accomplish. I say "what we do" instead of "what we *will* do" because the process is evolving and has been for some time. We are making you mindful of this now because you will it to be, as do I. So it is what we do. This is a fine example of creating a projected thought with intention for a united purpose. Through conscious will and agreement, we combine our projected thought of intent in truth and without interference of any kind.

Take a moment and fill it with the thought of the void, Original Thought and how it all began. In the process of this memory, you will begin to activate a dormant part of the brain that will assist you in receiving higher wisdom. It is a subtle shift. You are adjusting to the energy quite well and we are attempting to refine the input to reduce any discomfort you may experience. I ask that you greet the dawn and begin anew each day and be glad in your reflection. We have truly just begun. Go forth into the act of being and believe in the Self and it will bring you home.

*I have included Mother's closing to this day's message, as it helps to illustrate how vigilant and careful she always was in allowing me ample time to adjust to the increased energy flow that accompanied each succeeding session. I would be off to work soon after the close of each session and needed to ground myself in order to function in the world. As to the activation of that dormant part of my brain, I continue to wait for that light to go on as my life progresses and the messages continue.*

I feel it is time that you have a beginning to the story of who you are, and there is no better beginning than that of Original Thought. I have taken you back to the beginning of time, and to the spaces in between, to give you a picture of where it all began. Now that the picture is established in your mind, we may begin in earnest to discuss the importance of your own original thought. You will notice I did not have you capitalize the letters in referring to your personal original thought so that we may differentiate it from the Creator, where it all began. It is rather the same as referring

to the words "daughter" and "son" in relation to "Father" and "Mother."
You begin to understand.

When creation began, the vastness of space was organized into multiple
layers of similar creations existing in a number of dimensions scattered
about the universal order. When I asked you to go back to Original
Thought and all the spaces in-between, you began to understand my
meaning. I believe that it is essential for you to return often to the very
beginning in order to know and understand the origin of your being and
to have a starting point from which to measure your journey. You will
remember that I cautioned you to know from whence you came if you
were truly to know where you are going, so I have taken you back to this
beginning time and even beyond so that you may form a clear picture
in your human mind. All of mankind's lineage may be traced from this
beginning time; there are truly no "newbies" in your universe.

We have given the name Original Thought to our beginning because
it is just that—*original*—not to be duplicated or reproduced in any way.
It is an interesting concept to think that one can create scientifically
such distinctive life forms as the sparks from Original Thought. It is not
doable, although there are those who continue to try. I can only assume
that it is in some way an attempt to rise above the One who is your prime
creator. Why do I bring this up now? There are those who are continuing
to experiment in an attempt to produce life from other than the cells of
Original Thought. These attempts will fail eventually, but not before some
truly horrendous results are produced. These so-called "creations" will be
quickly destroyed and many profound lessons learned as a result. That is all
for now on this subject, but be content in the knowledge that the purity of
Original Thought can neither be tampered with nor denied.

Stand with me in the light of Original Thought and contemplate the
scenario that brought us to this place in time. I have provided you with
a window to gaze through in order to view all that has ever been until
this very moment in time. As we stand side-by-side and gaze out into the
vastness of time and space, we see the many layers and the spaces in between
as we merge and become One and then separate once more to pulse with
our own inner light being, our unique life force. Your story begins right
here and right now. This is an auspicious day, for we have removed the

cover from your eyes that will not see and from your ears that will not hear and opened your mind to free you from the limitations of your human form. We are sweeping out the cobwebs and clearing the decks for takeoff. This is where it all began, and it encompasses everything we have ever known to be the truth of our existence. The layers and dimensions you see go on forever and are without end, for creation can never be confined; it can only continue to evolve in each moment. Original Thought did not cease to be with the creation of this universal order. No, indeed, for the ebb and flow of creation is ever-expanding. There are some upon your planet who have knowledge of the layers and dimensions that are present and have learned to access them at will. They are known by many names in different cultures throughout history. Some are called oracles, prophets and psychics, to name but a few. Your little universe is an ever-expanding dot in the vastness of it all.

Through all the dimensional levels of your existence and all the layers of time, space and creation, you and I have come together like this to begin a journey that will uncover forgotten memories. These awakened memories will allow you to expand and go beyond the restrictions of this energy field and travel about the universe at will. For now, we ask only that you contemplate this and let it dwell within your mind as you go about your day. As you watch the rain begin to fall and see the earth washed clean, think of it as a great metaphor for your mind and your vision.

We have gone once more to the beginning. We have gazed upon the path we will walk—the path that looks familiar because we have walked this way before. We have looked at the void and found it teeming with life, energy and projected thoughts. Some of these thought patterns have been yours, and some have been the thoughts, dreams and ideas of others. When you visualize the void from the beginning, all the space you see before you is filled with the teeming life of multiple dimensions intersecting, running parallel and weaving around each other in a constant flow of movement. It is then you begin to realize the void is anything but empty.

You are the sparks from Original Thought imbued with the energy and drive to know the Self in this created form. It will always come back to the Self. What a beautiful and timeless gift you have been given! What a beautiful gift you are, mankind. You are life perpetuating itself, ever evolving, constantly planning, selflessly serving, illuminating and searching. You are the ever- eternal Self. It is where all paths begin. You have everything you need and are the spark from Original Thought, the child set upon the path of creation. You are life eternal, and I have taken you back so that you may begin to understand the uniqueness of the Self and the gift of life everlasting. Now you will learn to make the most of it. When you begin to accept that the Self is neither good nor evil, right or wrong, but simply *Is,* then you will start to comprehend a much broader picture than the one you have previously understood, or possibly never understood at all. When one accepts the idea of Original Thought, the spaces in between, and the void and the purpose of creation, then one begins to understand the concept of the Self and the opposites that are really not opposites at all. Come forth into the act of being and believe in the Self. It is the key to every new beginning and where you have placed yourself to be at this timing. Take heart in this knowledge, and be at peace.

# CHAPTER SEVEN

# THE HUMAN MIND

You are on a quest to unravel the truth from the lies—the true memory from that which has been planted in your cells—and to seek the light and pull it from the darkness. The quest we are on and the road we travel is one of discovery. What will be discovered or further revealed, may well knock the world on its behind, give it a good shake and much to contemplate. But for now, I would simply like you to take a moment and envision the life that you wish to live. Is it very different from the one you live now? What would you do if you could do or be anything you want, possess anything you desire? Think about this and give it your careful consideration.

Remember the stories of old, where the genie came out of the proverbial bottle to grant three wishes? If this happened today, what would you wish for? How would you wish to change your present life if you could have anything and everything that you now know to exist? Please pay attention to the little codicil that I placed at the very end of that thought—*that you now know to exist*—for that is truly the point of this exercise. Take the opportunity to step out of your box of limits for just a moment and ask yourself this question: "Do I really want what I ask this genie to manifest right now from my limited thoughts and perception?" Perhaps you will decide to wait a bit longer to have your every wish granted, until you can have a clearer, more unlimited picture of who you really are. If so, then it will be a very wise choice on your part. Have faith and trust that you will be nurtured and guided along the way.

You have opened yourself to be made aware of the truths that have lain dormant in your Soul and asked that they be revealed unto you. I have given you the key: Come forth into the act of being and believe in the Self. You have repeated it, contemplated its significance and begun to understand to the best of your ability. The meaning is simple. The truth always is. Ask yourself how you may *act* in the course of *being,* and then have faith that the Self and the belief in what is revealed in the process of coming forth will help you find your answers. When one believes in the Self, it implies a deeper understanding of what the Self has to reveal. Do you believe that you are that all-encompassing spark from Original Thought? Is the belief in the Self the beginning or the end of the journey? Can there even be an end to the journey? So many questions and a Pandora's Box has been opened into all possibility and truth. Would you have me answer all the questions for you now, or will you take the time to find some of these answers for yourself?

I will tell you a story of one simple man and his lifetime upon this planet. He was happy in his life, surrounded by loved ones, wealthy in coin and the richness of family and friends. He was respected, loved and honored for the way in which he lived. He was kind and generous in material goods, as well as in his generosity of Spirit. Why should a man such as this ever seek to find the key to belief in the Self? He had only to think upon a desire and it was granted. His lifetime contained everything he wished from the perspective of limited thought: love, good health, prosperity and happiness. This may be as far as one would wish to go on their path. Perhaps that is enough. Your wishes are granted. All is good. End of story. You are complete. I have only one question to ask: Have you found fulfillment such as this in your present lifetime? Do you have similar circumstances in your life and the same compassion that feeds your soul and makes you complete? If so, you may wish to read no further. You have created a wonderful existence and may use your current act of being to indulge in limited thought and be content. If that is your choice, then enjoy it, for there is no judgment here. However, if you wish to look further down the road, you will see that a door has been left open with the opportunity for you to step through it at anytime. Those of you who do so will be met by your guides, teachers and other beings of the light realm that are more than eager to walk beside you on your journey to discover all possibility and truth. Just for a moment, take a step through this door with me and visualize what lies beyond. Expand your consciousness and leave limited thought behind. Are you beginning to see the vast possibilities that are available to you? Through this door mankind is awakening. The debris of lifetimes is being lifted and the darkness is blending with the light and expanding into an infinite array of colors, sights and sounds. Savor this moment of discovery, for you are now in perfect alignment to feel and understand who it is that is being revealed and awakened within you.

Deep in the soul of mankind there resides a calling to come forth—a calling that brings to light the memory of all that has ever been and will ever be. There is a well of remembrance deep in your soul that never forgets. The quest you are on is to discover these truths. To "quest" is to search. Your quest will bring back the knowledge of the beginning when Original Thought was born and even before that time when there was only the void. It is your human mind that I seek to mold and to expand, for it is as much a part of you as your Soul. You have created your human mind through your journey. It is not your enemy as some might think, but it can be accessed to expand into the act of being and to align more closely with that of Original Thought. I have taken you back to the beginning and even before that, and to all the spaces in between, in order for your mind to accept what is being given. You understand now where this journey truly began and can look down the path from this perspective and know where we are headed. The human mind is an integral part of it. I have seen the books that are written and heard great teachers speak to you of moving out of your human mind to more clearly explore the Soul. This has proven to be an impossible task for most of you and not completely successful for those individuals who claim to have achieved it. The human mind is a fundamental part of the total human package and we will endeavor to help you understand, rather than ignore, its purpose.

The human mind was originally an experiment that was brought forth to your ancestors from these first inhabitants. Do you recall when I spoke earlier of those who passed through the golden disk and altered their molecular structure to align with the vibrational energy that would allow them to live here? I didn't elaborate at the time, but it was then that the human mind began to emerge. First, the thought was formed as a consequence of this successful passage, and then a projection of this thought was expanded. The human mind came about as the result. It was out of these newly projected thoughts that something quite unforeseen was created. These new beings found that they had been altered from pure Soul essence to a body with a mind as well as Spirit, and they judged what had been created. They continued to experiment, refine, create and eliminate what did not suit. They were much like newborns but fully grown, with remarkable powers. The human mind was formed, refined and created by the will of these playful gods. The mind was not an enemy of creation but a *part* of creation itself. As such, it was unleashed to develop through the will of those participants in the experiment called "inhabiting a new land." The human mind was not the enemy then, and it is not the enemy now. When this is fully realized and accepted, you can learn to harness what may seem to be the negative aspects of human mind and encourage the growth of the more positive aspects.

You have continued to develop methods for moving out of the human mind and more into the Spirit mind and are learning to do this quite well. It is important for you to acknowledge and accept that you are never completely free of the human mind as long as you are attached to the body you have come to inhabit. However, since you now know it is not your enemy, you can relax a bit more and allow it to be. Only then can you learn to bend it to your will, for your will is stronger. The mind was created by your will to quest and to know and to survive here on terra. Are you beginning to understand a bit more? Because the human mind is your creation, it can be altered at will.

Now that we have dispelled the notion of the mind as something you must conquer, you can embrace it as part of the reason you reside here and part of the reason you were able to survive. Those adventurers who passed through the golden disk of vibrational energy are your ancestors, known to you as the ancient ones who made your existence here possible in the first place. There are those who reside deep in the caves of the Himalayas even now and have continued to monitor what has come to pass in this adventure and experiment called "planet earth." It has been an ongoing project for many billions of years. When I speak of billions of years in terms that you understand, you may not be able to fathom this expanse of time. For those of us who travel freely between universes, several billion years is nothing because time is not limited for us, nor is space. We know ourselves to be infinite and so can travel from place to place in a blink of an eye. Your planet has been a critical part of our journey and we have come often to watch you evolve. I have heard your many thoughts concerning what mankind has wrought upon this beautiful planet, and it is true that, at times, experimentation and destruction seems rampant. I will tell you this: your planet will not be destroyed but will continue to evolve as it moves into its natural state of rebirth.

What some of you are learning is that rebirth does not have to come about through destruction but rather through great knowledge, experimentation and creation from Source. Rebirth is an evolutionary process, for nothing is ever truly destroyed, only expanded. Those heinous perpetrators of evil upon the earth—the Hitlers and other evil doers of your history—were not destroyed, but upon their passing given the opportunity to expand their being to become closer to the Source of all truth and love. It is the way of what you call "heaven" to take the human mind and to expand it and bring it closer to the Source. Now you have it. The human mind is taken off the list of enemies to be overcome and, instead, is acknowledged as a sign of humanity's development, part and parcel of the whole package, created right along with everything else by your adventurers and travelers through time. Let us move on and go forth into the act of being.

The human mind, with all its folly, is really rather a unique and interesting subject for study. My scribe is awakened at 4:00 AM because this represents what we are studying and learning about accessing all the spaces in between. At this early hour, you live between darkness and the dawn. The space in between the two is like its own time/space continuum. It is a good metaphor and one you can relate to, as you learn that you don't only reside in a world of black or white or good or evil, you also live and exist in the spaces in between these opposites as well. There are those who have occupied the spaces in between from the beginning of their human existence. While this expanded awareness has been difficult for them at times, it has also allowed a broader vision and acceptance of universal truths. They bring lost wisdom back into the conscious minds of those who have forgotten and further their return to true purpose.

We acknowledge that your human life can become easily consumed by daily living and trying to maintain the Self in this limited world, but we are committed to waking up the human mind to the awareness of the spaces in between your conscious and unconscious existence. The human mind plays a pivotal role in this discovery. Shall I tell you how? The human mind functions as your bellwether and temperature gage and entertains you when you might go mad from your attempts to fit in. It maintains your desire to learn and keeps you balanced while living the human condition. The human mind does not keep you from searching for something more, but it helps you to maintain sanity while you do so. It is quite fascinating to watch the balancing act that exists at just about every level of your so-called "waking life" on this planet. It is the human mind that allows you to find the opposites of which we speak. It is the human mind that puts up the mirror so you may gaze into it and see beyond your reflection as human. It is the human mind that steps aside willingly to allow you to sip from the knowledge of that which lies beyond it. It is the human mind that covers your soul until such time as the truth may be revealed. It is the human mind that stops you when you venture too far and then acts as a barrier to shield the information from overpowering what you are currently able to absorb. It gives you a gauge in which to measure these drops of truth and then dispense them so they may be absorbed more quickly and with greater ease. You soon begin to see the importance of the human mind in all that we do together.

The human condition is such that there are some humans who cannot consciously monitor and adjust the flow of information bombarding them. As a result they become severely out of balance and may be termed mentally ill. They are unable to filter the information for one reason or another and the knowing becomes too great. The human mind cannot always assist one such as this, for they have delved too deeply into other realms of existence and are unable to maintain the balance of the soul mind with the human mind. The world would call them "mad," and we would say they are "out of balance." In your medical communities there are treatment methods evolving that will assist them to blend more completely the soul mind with the human mind and help them find true balance. Great teachers are bringing such information now, and articles have already been written about some of these methods. This new information will gain more prominence in the future, and you will hear of it in your media.

At the beginning of life, as a baby just formed, you were nurtured in the womb of mother and birthed into the world. And there you were, completely at the mercy of those around you for the care and nurturing of your soul, your body and your developing mind. It is a painful fact that not all newly born on this planet are given such nurturing. There may be some who are brutalized, ignored or treated unfairly. As a result, very little balance is achieved and the baby grows up with a much different awareness than one who is allowed to develop in safety. You have seen the behavior that this type of upbringing can produce. However, these humans can also shed their human condition of pain and suffering and find their balance and thrive. There are those of you who are bringing information to the forefront that will help to make it easier for such growth to occur.

It is fascinating to observe how mankind has evolved and developed the Spirit with the human mind, and the unique balance maintained between them. As a direct result, the ability to think and reason is expanded. For example, while my scribe is in the process of writing these missives and still present in her human mind, the Spirit comes upon her and she is in perfect balance to receive. As she transcribes what is given, she sits and allows this soul or spirit mind to receive, while keeping the human or conscious mind off to one side but still present. The human mind then becomes the observer and, as such, is able to learn right along with the Spirit mind. Neither the human mind nor the Spirit mind is to be denied when the process is reversed. The end result is a proper melding or merging of the two to form a more perfect union of awareness, ability and illuminated condition. It has already been achieved by some known as "master teachers" or "illumed beings" living in complete balance. They are the examples of which I speak and where you will find your peace. It is from this state of balance that your ability to create at will is made possible. The human mind is not an enemy to be tucked away when you are exploring your truth but needs to be embraced in order to grow and develop.

Soul mind and human mind, having separate functions and abilities, must combine in order to serve the human condition. Only then will you achieve the balance that enables complete forward motion to occur. When you repeat the mantra, "Come forth into the act of being and believe in the Self," all the various aspects of your soul essence are brought forth into balance and alignment. You will be reminded to come forth into the act until it is no longer an "act" but your true state of balance at all times. Use this phrase to remember balance and peace. When you are in balance, all things flow in perfect harmony; but when you are not, your world seems fragmented and you become stressed in mind, body and Spirit. It is my continued prayer that you will achieve this perfect balance and find the peace of your existence.

# CHAPTER EIGHT

# CREATING THE CONSCIOUS MIND

The conscious mind, the ego or human mind is the one that allows you to judge yourself and the life you lead. It is the one that assists you in the creation of your box of limits and takes you out of the need for deeper examination of any esoteric or unexplained experiences. In point of fact, it explains them away quite nicely. The conscious mind enables you to function within the realm of "human" in your day-to-day existence. Conscious mind was not always as it is today. When first we moved out from the caves of learning, we had only the one mind. We were aware of our beginning and of Original Thought. As sparks with the memory of Source, we went out into the void to populate the universal order. We projected our thoughts and became creators... until it began to change. We realized that our pure thoughts and intent to create were being unwittingly and negatively influenced by the thoughts of others. In our innocence, we were surprised to learn that this subtle weaving of interrelated thought patterns had been occurring over many lifetimes and through countless experiences. It was a time of great introspection and change in how we used our projected thought to create.

It was at this time that we devised the concept of the "conscious mind" to include group mind as well as individual thought. Our awareness of this group mind consciousness allowed us to move forward with our thought projections while still maintaining control of the outcome. At the same time, continuing to acknowledge that Original Thought existed, we advanced our ability for group awareness and cooperation. In order to maintain a counter balance for conscious mind and sustain a direct connection to Original Thought, we continued developing our Spirit, or "unconscious mind." This was our link to Original Thought and to the origins of our birth. We learned to divide our thought patterns into these two distinct minds: the human *conscious*, and the Spirit or unconscious mind, also known as the *subconscious*. There have been problems along the way, and you have only to look at the world past and present to see that very few humans seem to be operating in balance of these two minds. You will remember my stating that conscious mind is often subject to group manipulation and requires closer scrutiny. While beautiful and uplifting thoughts have been created from this group mind consciousness, there have also been wars, famine, disease and prejudice. You may well ask where the unconscious mind is in this so-called "evolutionary process." I would tell you it is there, minding its own business, waiting to be accessed more often. The populating of this planet was a grand experiment and we were able to learn a great deal from the experience. We continue to observe the results of this initial adventure and have come back often to monitor and, in some instances, help mankind to evolve a better way to proceed. We have attempted to present the importance of coming forward with the two minds operating in balance through the teachings of countless sages, scholars and enlightened men and women throughout your history, who have spread the word. However, the conscious mind has continued to reign supreme, with the spirit mind—the unconscious source of Original Thought—accessed rarely. Well, I think it's time that was changed!

Some of you might feel you can operate with one mind or the other quite nicely and need no interference. You have determined that you are in complete balance and harmony and are living quite nicely in the process, thank you very much. What we have observed, however, is that when you lose sight of the ability and intent of Original Thought for even one moment, you can no longer fully connect and maintain the balance between the two. You forget your true purpose, and chaos reigns. What you feel you know or have read about the conscious and subconscious mind is not enough; you must, in reality, do something with these insights in order to bring about a more stable planet and a more peaceful life. What is our purpose now? We have many, but the one I offer at this time puts forth the intention to create one mind from the two. As a result, you will take the best of both and combine them. To achieve this goal, think of the merged minds as true consciousness, or True Mind, if you will. *True,* because it is directly linked with Original Thought, the unconscious or spirit connection; and *Mind*, the conscious and more limited part of the equation. You combine these two to form True Mind and fully connect to Original Thought, which is pure and free of interpretation because it is original. It is your beginning, and True Mind will always remember that beginning. The conscious mind enters into the True Mind by bringing forth an understanding of group thought.

It is important that the conscious and unconscious are both recognized as vital to the balance of your existence here. There are some planets outside your immediate solar system that operate exclusively within the realm of Original Thought and some that operate only through the conscious mind. The difference in their evolutionary development is painfully clear. We came from a planet that operates completely in sync with Original Thought. That idea is relatively new here but is not without precedence elsewhere. There are a few very ancient planets in this universal order that operate fully in balanced mind consciousness, or what we call True Mind. On these planets there is total peace and the continuing exploration and expansion of universal truths as they relate to Original Thought. For those of you who are willing and ready to explore and to exist within this state of being, now is the opportunity to do so. True Mind is not only a concept for your future but also the memory of your origin. It can be accomplished by transforming one conscious thought after another into True Mind consciousness. "Come forth into the act of being" can be a beginning of this process and the catalyst for further connection to occur. Let's take one thought—for example, *I am angry at my father*—and transform this one thought into true spirit- mind connection. You might say:

> "I am angry with my father, who is who I am. I am at peace within my anger. I am healed within my anger. I am at peace. I Am."

Can your anger at your father be dissipated so easily? Well, perhaps not so easily at first. Remember, we are only just beginning to practice this convergence of two minds, and I have shown you only a very simple example. It is a thought process that one goes through. *What is faithfully projected into your thoughts will become manifest.* Though this may not be a new concept for some of you, the merging of these two minds will help you create a world of individual peace while continuing to live consciously within your structured society. As a result, everything around you will change and a new world order will begin to emerge. Take your random thoughts, talk them through from a spirit-mind perspective, combine them into True Mind, and experience a state of oneness and True Mind consciousness. Your journey doesn't stop there but only brings you to another adventure. True Mind captures a thought from your human consciousness and prepares it to blend with spirit-mind in a never-ending dance of reality. This new reality is created totally by you and for you, separate from anything you have accomplished thus far. In True Mind, one is able to create lifetimes in which all paths lead to happiness and fulfillment of purpose. This is a motivation that permeates your world. So many books in the Western world deal with subjects from creating your own reality to being happy and fulfilled throughout your life. It is a focus of many and achieved by relatively few—not even entirely by those few, either. At this time, we will not delve into the multitude of theories and methods presented to find this elusive happiness but instead will resurrect a very ancient method of achieving just such a goal. Simply stated, *true happiness comes from True Mind experience and the conscious awareness of this perfected state of being.* Can it be that simple? If so, why hasn't it been shared till now? Well, because it is being shared at this moment, in the perfect time for its arrival. In the caves of learning, when we operated from projected thought to create new life, the results were often not to our liking. Some of the mythical creatures of ancient lore were created in such a manner and rejected when the interfering thought projections of others were discovered to be tainted and not purely from True Mind consciousness. We learned to focus our thought projections only through the True Mind so we could successfully perfect our intentions. We were given all the tools and knowledge we required to create in this fashion and live in True Mind consciousness.

In the true spirit of experimentation and perfecting of Original Thought on this planet, the True Mind was separated into conscious and subconscious awareness. We observed how man created, utilizing these two minds. Before long, what began to happen was a gradual eroding of the balance and harmony between the two. The conscious mind soon became the driving force, and the spirit mind—the unconscious—became that vague state of being achieved rarely and with great effort. The conscious mind became a dominant, driving force for humanity, and True Mind, quite literally, became a thing of the past.

You are being awakened now to acknowledge your connection to Original Thought, which can be accomplished through living the True Mind experience. It is a state of being that must survive, and the universal order of the void requires that this occur now. True Mind is achieved when one becomes aware that it's possible. Take time to contemplate this. It is important and necessary to begin to merge the two seemingly separate consciousnesses. I say "seemingly separate" because it was an experiment from the beginning, and an illusion, if you will, of the true state of being. In order to correct this illusion, we must bring together the creative force of the conscious and unconscious mind that has been allowed to exist in apparent separation. Original Thought is our natural state of being, and True Mind the goal. True Mind will allow you to come back to the original state of being and no longer live in the illusion of limit and separation. True Mind will bring you peace as you begin to see clearly, without interference, the way in which you create. You are not at the whim of someone else's reality unless you allow it. You may ask why some people live in poverty, pain or rejection. To answer that question, remember what has been said about the focus of projected group thought on the creation of your reality. For example, throughout the ages a state of fear has been maintained through a collection of thought patterns that "agree" with the creation of disasters, disruptions of the social order and crimes beyond imagining. Global warming is on your news media often and is an example of collective thought projections created from millions of focused thoughts on just this scenario. You will be taken step-by-step, awareness-by-awareness, experience-by-experience until you can begin to see the importance of creating projected thoughts upon your screen of reality only from the pure essence of the True Mind. You will come forth into the act of being as this perfected thought, and you will believe in the Self enough to know that it is so. I do not give you false information but seeds to plant. These seeds of thought and awareness will lead you to discover True Mind once more. Before this can happen, you must become consciously aware of what is occurring now. Educating yourself to the reality of group manifestation is an important first step. From a perspective of observation, look clearly at what is occurring on your planet—both the beauty as well as the tragedy, for they are very much a part of your life. To bring about change, one must see clearly. And that is your assignment for now.

As the observer, you must remove yourself as much as possible from the outcome and allow an opening to occur so that Original Thought can come forth into True Mind and life as you know it will change. Do not be impatient. Find where you have the least patience and remove yourself a little to observe and discover the origin of this impatience. I will be surprised if a state of fear is not present somewhere in the equation, but that will be your discovery to make. I project my thought patterns into yours for purposeful good until you can stand once more on your own. This is not a totally solitary journey. Know that mankind enjoys the company of others, and that you will not be isolated but only more aware and conscious and in tune with your Original Thought and True Mind reality. This is a very good place to be and one from whence you came originally.

The adventure is coming full circle. You are here for the revelation of discovery and are creating, from your own knowledge, a new, yet very ancient, state of being. I caution you to take care of yourself in the physical. Rest, play, laugh, contemplate and come forth into the act of being what you have come here to be. You are the creators of the universal order. Create from knowledge of the Self. It is a beginning, always a beginning, and let that be enough for now. Take only small steps, as you are in the act of creation. It is a wondrous place to be, and we will do this from awareness of the past, which is simply the future recreating itself. You will understand this in many layers. Be happy in your day and be the observer. The only thing that will ever change is your perspective of the Self. Observe this without judgment of right or wrong, good or bad, but from a place of resolve to see clearly and allow all things in accordance with your state of awareness. You will begin to expand in ways you never could have imagined until now.

# CHAPTER NINE

# EMBRACING ONE TRUE MIND

The Spirit, or unconscious mind, has maintained the connection to Original Thought from the beginning of human existence. In the process of evolution, it has become an unconscious state of being. The spirit-mind is the place of all-knowing and the connection to the One. It is from this place that you are able to access the wisdom of the ages. It is here that the ability to create is born and the sparks that have lain dormant for lifetimes are ignited. The fire is always banked and continues to burn slowly in the spirit-mind, waiting with great anticipation for the conscious mind to reconnect once more as True Mind. These separate minds—the conscious and the subconscious—have caused mankind to live in a duplicitous state.

The original purpose for the conscious mind was to be a support for the unconscious mind and to assist in mankind's development. It was never intended to take over and supersede the Spirit, or unconscious mind. The creation of the conscious mind became a significant learning experience and one that has yet to be resolved to satisfaction. If mankind is once again to embrace the one True Mind, these two separate entities must be joined as one. This may prove to be a difficult task, but it is not impossible. For our purpose, I will continue to identify the two minds, the conscious and unconscious, as "entities." When these entities have become one True Mind, there is no thought of separation and no memory of the dominion of one over the other. I have spoken of the purpose of this merging so that you can have a more complete picture and understanding of Original Thought. If you are that spark from Original Thought—and you most certainly are—why must you exist with two separate minds that are often divided in purpose and direction? Your seeming separation from Original Thought has caused some confusion, and in order to bring you what you truly desire you must operate from one True Mind. Operating from True Mind brings such clarity that you will see the outcome of projected thought made manifest as if on a screen before you. Stepping out of the pattern you have lived in for so many lifetimes and embracing a new way of thinking and believing may not be easy, but it is important to contemplate. In order to continue, you must take each step as presented. You must know when it is time to plant the seed and water the garden, and when it is time to pull the weeds of doubt. Only then may you step back and watch the magnificent flowers grow. True Mind can be thought of as your "blossoming flower"—the beauty that you seek, and the peace that comes from ownership of the Self. True Mind will enable you to create from the source of Original Thought once more, as was always intended. This is an opportune time to bring back this knowledge to this little dot in the universal order called planet Earth. The *how* of this achievement will be taught in many layers. Coming from your current belief in two minds and through your progression into the reality of one mind, you will gain new insights and the peace that you seek. Some insights may literally take your breath away as you begin to operate more from within this informed awareness.

Now, back to how you may begin to merge the conscious and unconscious into the one True Mind. Capture a limited thought from your conscious mind, examine this thought and then change it: *I have no money in the bank*, a limited thought from the perspective of the conscious mind, becomes *I have abundant funds in the bank to see to my comfort*, which is an unlimited belief from the subconscious mind. So, you speak your thoughts and create what you want without limit. It doesn't matter if you don't fully believe it as yet, or you think it is a pointless exercise; it is simply a place for you to begin. This effortless exercise initially creates confusion in the conscious mind, which becomes off balance and, thus, more easily influenced by Spirit. Every thought that is limited you must turn around and speak in positive terms. Remember, you are in the process of building trust and peeling away the many layers of limited thought, and the results you desire may not come instantly. The goal of this exercise is to understand how we arrived at the two separate minds in the first place and then begin to change it.

At first, you may find it very difficult to identify what your limited thoughts are. Some of these thoughts are so habitual and ingrained in your conscious mind that when seen by you may not seem limited at all. Pick one that you know is a glaring example and begin. Identify and observe your limited thought and bring it into unlimited, positive expression. *I can never lose weight* becomes *my body maintains a weight that is perfect for me*. It can be this simple. You may perceive this to simply be an affirmation, but it goes far beyond the act of affirming; it makes inroads into the beliefs of your limited conscious mind. What I ask is that you begin to open to the possibility that two minds can live as one in truth. When these thoughts have merged, true creation happens. You cannot create abundantly from separation. It is not possible.

What is the purpose of the unconscious mind? This intelligence, directly connected to Spirit, comes to us from the truth of Original Thought. It remembers everything that has been and all that shall be. Its purpose is to remember what has been forgotten, so the spirit-mind—the intelligence of the unconscious—needs to be made conscious once more. If your spirit-mind connection becomes once again the True Mind reality, you may well ask why you need to be in this third-dimensional, limited world at all. You may have a valid point. Why would you choose to be limited when you can remember it all? In answer to this question I would simply say, it is for the opportunity to learn and grow.

Your Spirit, the subconscious, is not a static entity. It is ever-growing and expanding, much like the universal All. The conscious mind wants to maintain what it considers to be the status quo. It was not intended to be anything more than a counterbalance to All That Is, and was in no way to supersede the growth or function of the spirit-mind. What happened, in actuality, was that the conscious/ego mind developed into something that maintained the status quo and the spirit-mind became nothing more than a vague whisper that was difficult to access. Ego, or conscious mind, began to reign supreme, leaving little room for the Spirit to operate, or so it would seem. The creation and further development of the two minds was an experiment. The original intention was that the two would forever function in tandem, working together, aware of each other while continuing to change and grow. That was the plan, anyway. At the time, we did not foresee the outcome (this is why it was called an experiment) and what, in reality, developed over time were two distinctively separate minds. So, here we are back in the caves of learning, reassessing our handiwork. It is not my purpose to tell you that what developed was wrong, but I ask you to consider it truthfully. Conscious mind has served you well, but you are seeking the truth that is only available through the unconscious spirit-mind. For far too long, your conscious mind has determined this truth for you. As a result of that limit, there have been distortions on an individual as well as global scale. Conscious, or ego mind, has purported to help or protect you by superseding spirit-mind and presenting this limited vision as truth. Spirit-mind simply waits for that truth to be revealed. Your only enemy is complacency and doubt of your connection to Spirit. When you are able to speak truth through these simple affirmations, the conscious mind begins to blend with Spirit, and the unconscious becomes consciousness as One. The important and vital purpose for these exercises is to change limited thought. It is not a simple request that I ask of you. Take small steps and become the observer for the many events in your life. If you came to this lifetime to find truth from a new and untried perspective, then here is your opportunity to do so. You have never been at the whim of creation; you were always the creator and part of the process.

We have watched you through lifetimes, and you frequently end up in the same place, embracing limited thought. We want to help you change this life cycle just a bit. Do not be content to relive your past lives in an attempt to find answers. They are the past and never to be repeated. You are on the path moving toward a new acknowledgement of the Self. You are about the business of finding the truth and no longer living these dual identities of conscious and unconscious minds. It is the combining of these two into one that must take precedence. You are on a quest to return to Original Thought and the truth that will flow from this knowledge. When you begin creating from this truth and alignment with the One, your expanded mind— the Spirit consciousness—will enlighten your soul. You must continually ask yourself what it is that you want. The answer will determine your journey's direction. Do not answer this question quite yet; instead, give it the contemplation that it requires. What do you want? It is a deceptively simple query and yet perhaps the most difficult to answer right now. Be the honest observer of your life on both a personal and global scale, but always through non-judgmental eyes. The honest contemplation of this question will lead you to insights only you can set into motion.

How, then, does one go about creating from one True Mind? You have been asked to be the observer, and I have watched you go about your day and how you relate to the world around you. I have been an observer of your planet and its inhabitants from the beginning of your evolution. I am joined now with many others of the light realm in an attempt to find the spark that will ignite the banked fire of True Mind into full flame. This is why I have asked you to be the observer and lay the foundation upon which to build this truth. Answering the question, "What do I want?" will be one of the key elements to the successful merging of the two minds and will determine the success of your adventure. Finding what you want will become a place of total creative focus and unlimited Original Thought. It is the path that will lead you home. Initially, when you asked yourself the question, "What do I want?" the answers may have included immediate gratification, more wealth, a true love, good health, and so forth. When given some time to think upon it, your answers may be more altruistic, as in "world peace." Do you want a cure for cancer or an end to poverty? It may well be that when the genie is let out of the bottle, you would be more magnanimous in your desires. Before you answer this question, take the time to be the observer of your present-day life, job, family, acquaintances, etc. Observe it all. If you wish, your observations can even include a more global perspective. Do not overwhelm yourself with your observations, but in the course of your day, pay attention to what is around you. Most of you have forgotten how to observe, how to really focus on the world that has been created from these two coexisting minds, and as a result, some interesting insights may occur for you. More and more, your spirit-mind will begin to seep through into your limited consciousness. It can't help but happen in this way. Not only will you be the observer of what lies on the surface but you will begin to see and understand the many layers and dimensional properties that make up your current life expression. You will see around the edges and in between the lines and through the time and space of limit. This may happen in an instant. The unconscious mind will register these insights and begin to make inroads into the conscious mind, and then expansion will occur. You will be putting into action the mantra *Come forth into the act of being*. It will be an *act* until it becomes a part of who you are in totality. Right now you are acting upon all the things that will take you back to the reality of *being*.

For now, be the observer. Contemplate what you want and go forth unto your day with the insight you gain. Do not analyze as yet. Just relax into the observations as you go about your day. What we ask is not difficult. The effort you put into awakening instead of sleep- walking through your life will help you immensely in accepting and integrating the work to come. You are multi-dimensional beings; you always have been. Start to use the many heightened abilities that enhance your awareness to be the observer, but don't forget to observe yourself as well. I caution you to focus and, through that focus, see the many layers that exist in your life. The multiple layers and dimensional properties that make up your life may come to your awareness in a flash of recognition, or it may take some time before you see clearly. Do not judge it either way. Make a commitment with the Self that on this day, for an hour, a minute or whatever time you choose, you will look with eyes that do not see and listen with ears that do not hear the deeper layers of human existence. You are the observer, and in the process you will become more focused. This is a gradual practice and, in most cases, may not be realized consciously. That is the point. The spirit-mind is coming forth into consciousness and becoming True Mind.

Be the observer without preconceived judgment of the observation. Can you do it? Of course you can. Hold this thought: *I will go forth unto my day focused and observing of all things.* Make this your starting point and then forget about it. Let the Spirit, the unconscious mind, do its work. You have seeded the garden, now go toil in the fields of your life and see the fruits of your labor. It is a focus you will have from now on, and it will not change. We will be observing also. It is what we do and what you will do. Then and only then will you be able to answer the question "What do I want?" with any kind of accuracy.

# CHAPTER TEN

# THE CONSCIOUS OBSERVER

Becoming the conscious observer, with the mind focused outside the Self, you will begin to understand the world and your place in it. You already register countless amounts of information throughout your day, both on the conscious and unconscious level, and form certain judgments and beliefs as a result. As a conscious observer of the events and the people in your life for a minute, an hour or even sporadically throughout your day, you can expect to discover some important truths. One truth, *You are all Divine,* sparks from Original Thought presently masquerading as humans and carries a promise to come forth into the act of being and live your life accordingly. The insights you gain from being the observer will help you see and understand the many diverse layers of the Self that exist. As the conscious observer, you will have a more complete understanding of the concept "the act of being," which contains many layers of insight integrated and woven into one. Discovering these layers is much like untangling a knotted thread. First you find where the knot begins. Then start the unraveling, step by step, until the act of being is revealed in its entirety. You may not fully understand all you discover at the time, but you are being called upon to act anyway. And through your commitment to finding the truth that lies within the act of being, you will begin to see the Self more clearly. It is that simple.

We have spoken about the two minds becoming one True Mind and operating from this understanding. We have journeyed to the caves of learning, and examined the concepts of a clean slate and those of creating your life and the many events yet to come. I have given you the key to open the door to further discovery. "Come forth into the act of being and believe in the Self" is a simple phrase, painless to repeat, but perhaps not so easily understood. In order for you to experience a deeper understanding, we have given you a simple assignment: Pay attention to the Self. Pay attention, through focused observation, to the world around you. It is time to stop moving about your day like robots and wake up to your Spirit-Soul, your true being, and become a full participant in your life.

Step aboard my rocket ship for a minute and observe your planet from a more universal perspective. You are here, a mere dot in the universal order—though a most intriguing and beautiful one, to be sure! You have oceans and rivers, plants and animals, food in abundance and everything needed to sustain life as you know it to be. The gravitational pull of your planet helps to keep you grounded, and your conscious mind, in collaboration with the unconscious mind, keeps you moving forward, building, creating and evolving. From recorded history you learn from what has occurred in the past. Take the time to examine the present, and have hope for the future because you are the future. What is achieved today and what will be accomplished tomorrow will be brought forth from these contemplations. You are experiencing life, but at the same time being asked to drink from the cup of ancient wisdom, very ancient wisdom indeed. Learn from the limits and the mistakes of the past, remember the spark of your origin and live that realization more through your seeking.

When you are asked to become a more focused and committed observer, you might assume the sole purpose to be a deeper understanding of your life experience. To a certain extent, you would be correct. But another far more important reason is to have the ability to become Self-actualized. When you become Self-actualized through these focused observations, you become an active participant—not a spectator—in this play called your life. Through these observations you begin to have a greater understanding of your actions and reactions as they relate to your life expression. As a result, you become a Self-actualized being in a human body. Your journey is about the Self and being fully present in every moment.

To understand what it means to be fully present as a Self-actualized being, you may look to the journey of certain master teachers who are committed to being completely focused in the act of being. These Self-actualized

Masters come to teach what they know but are also committed "conscious observers" in order to gain wisdom and experience. Often, what happens for their students is viewed as less significant in the Masters' ultimate quest for Self-realization and growth. The truth of the teachers' personal quest is not always revealed to the students because it may appear to be egocentric and self-serving. But the fact remains that their primary purpose, as is yours, is to learn about the Self. It is only through your limited understanding that these Masters may appear selfish and self-absorbed.

At times a student's response to the teachings of these Masters can be very dogmatic. A strict adherence to their specific teaching is believed to be the only way to live and gain wisdom. The student may completely give himself over to the *act* of the master teacher and, in so doing, completely miss the true meaning of their message. The master teachers are here for Self growth, and there is much they can teach you. They may appear in many guises throughout your lifetime and are here to teach what they know and to gain in the process. It is up to you to integrate the wisdom they bring and make it real for you in such a way that you also grow in the process. Do not put your faith in the largess of the master teacher. If they are worth anything at all, they are here as you are, to gain further wisdom in order to perpetuate the growth of the Self. You may even become the master teacher for others at some point in your quest.

When I ask you to become the conscious observer, I want you to gain insight into the interactions and relationships of the Self to outside influences This is what a master teacher is forever experiencing. In order to become such a master, you must grow rapidly in this knowledge and rid yourself of what no longer serves you. A Master never stops learning and integrates what is learned "into the act of being." But first he willingly comes forth and takes advantage of every opportunity to learn and experience, as will you through the exercise of conscious observation. I come to you as a Master teacher so I may learn. In the process, I will teach so you may learn. And you will pass on the teachings so others may learn. And the circle of life continues. We will not build a church, because you can never remain static in your quest for Self-actualization. The universe is ever-growing and expanding and never fixed, and you are a necessary part of the universal order—a Divine spark from Original Thought. I am the teacher, you are the student. Then I am the student and you are the teacher. Our circle of wisdom is growing and expanding as it should. You have opened yourself to receive this teaching, and now you must contemplate and integrate the wisdom while continuing to move forward.

In your observation of human actions and reactions, you may see your reflection in the commonality shared within these experiences. Through the contemplation of what you observe, issues you've yet to resolve can be illuminated. What a Pandora's Box this opens as you begin to realize that everything encountered in your life has meaning and is your creation. It is true that there are many crimes committed toward individuals, families and even whole countries. You might ask why anyone would purposely create fear, injury and degradation in their life. I will tell you how this can happen.

The projected thoughts of a collective consciousness, when brought together and influenced by a group-mind belief, can bring about a multitude of challenges. Every day you are witness to this group-mind mentality, encouraged and shaped by the news media as well as influential organizations and governments. Group consciousness can bring about a pecking order, if you will, of those that "have" and those that "have naught," the rich and privileged and the poor and disenfranchised. It will also touch upon those who will be the victims and the ones who will victimize them. This pecking order can be created and justified through a group-mind consciousness that embodies the specific beliefs of a society. As the projected thoughts of group consciousness continue to interfere, the devastation that results can hinder your ability to experience full Self-realization.

The projected thoughts of group consciousness can become twisted in the one who commits violence on another. To say injury of any kind is for purposeful good and not just for the experience is highly inaccurate. To believe that any spark from Original Thought is destined to receive or to be responsible for violence, or to experience lack of any kind, is incorrect. And yet this is a belief that has been accepted far longer than your history has been recorded. It is simply not so. In order to counteract this collective consciousness belief, or any such belief system, you will have to more closely examine the truths you live now. It is this systematic inspection of your thought patterns and beliefs that has been set in motion through these teachings. As a result, you will begin to peel away the layers of deceit and misinformation little by little. What is revealed may at times be raw, hurtful and difficult to look upon, but look upon it anyway. You have made a good start. Now we will continue to unravel the knots in the threads that have brought you to this place in time. You will examine certain accepted truths brought about by the group collective consciousness, observe them more closely and dispose of what no longer brings you closer to the realized Self. It is through your observations that the Self is revealed. The journey now becomes one of stepping out of the beliefs of group consciousness and embracing the purpose of Original Thought, which is the realized Self. It is just a small step to be sure, but a step nonetheless.

The observation and examination of truth, as you perceive it, may be influenced by the beliefs of group consciousness. But judgment is not part of the consciousness of the True Mind or of the Self. You are preparing, as a fully realized human, for the truthful examination of the Self. In the meantime, lead your life every day as if you were the only Original Thought in the universe that had fully awakened. As this awakened spark of Original Thought, your realized Self will be taken out of storage and brushed off like a long-forgotten cloak. Try it on, this cloak of the Self, and see how it feels. Though the truth of this practice may last only a moment, it may be enough to have you wear that cloak more often and live the experience of a Self-actualized being. In your meditations or quiet contemplations, take some time and go back into the caves of learning as they have been described, and practice projecting on your life screen what you envision Original Thought would place there. When you are asked to come forth into the act of being in an exercise such as this, you are *acting* the part of Original Thought until such time as you remember it all. The truth of your projected life force will then be revealed, as the veil of forgetfulness begins to lift from your eyes.

You are being given an opportunity to evolve into something Original Thought never could have envisioned. You have learned and experienced life from the place of group consciousness and yet chosen the adventure of a new path and the direction that Original Thought will lead you. You have been the dark circle in the center of the light, as seen in the symbol of the yin and yang. This symbol aptly illustrates the opposites of darkness and light that are separate, yet still remain part of each other. This is who you have been and what you have journeyed in the universal order. Your experiences have been rich and varied, but it is time to come back to the full light of your being. By coming home to the realization of all that you are, you will begin to pull the darkness more into the light by your seeking.

Even before the caves of learning, you were the recognized sparks from the All. I continue to take you back to that realization so you may remember and come forth into True Mind consciousness without separation. You are being asked to journey as One thought and One mind and bring that realization once more to this planet. And by your commitment to journey this path, you begin to light the spark of ancient wisdom. The reactive thought patterns that surround you are not who you are. The life that you experience is not only yours by choice but also by the choice of an imposed group consciousness allowed through ignorance of that influence. Now, as you become stronger in the knowledge of who you are in truth, you can begin to change it. As the observer, you begin to live more fully in the True Mind experience by recognizing, without judgment, the influence of group consciousness in your life. Do not become overwhelmed in the process, but do this at first for brief moments of time in quiet contemplation and integrate these realizations in peace. It will be a time of great learning. Give up the need to rage against what you can easily change or fight what brings you peace. Do not attempt to vindicate your past life by resistance to the truth when it is revealed. It is time to move forward and to leave behind what does not serve you. Nothing is gained from holding on to ignorance. Our purpose is not to overwhelm you but to open the door just a bit more as you begin to integrate thought patterns that will lead you to greater discoveries. When you go about your day, be at peace and let this peace surround you. Greet each dawn with a new image of the rising sun and use this as a metaphor for the expansion of the Spirit within you. As you bless each day, always remember to also honor and celebrate your life.

# CHAPTER ELEVEN

# TRUE MIND AND TRUE BODY

Billions of years ago, those of us who came to inhabit your world made a commitment to experience the birth of an emerging planet where we could populate and create new life forms. We discovered that some of our projected thought creations were intermingled and that this unintentional interference had caused certain problems. Our dedication to observing, learning and then adapting what we had learned brought us significant insight into the Self. And this is what I have asked of you—to be the observer and expand Self-realization. You may feel you are close to understanding but never quite grasping the full knowledge of the truths that have been shared. You have been told to observe and contemplate your life from a new understanding and then to journey these insights, often without a clear destination in view. I have shared with my scribe, as I now share with you, mankind, that the trust that is built between us must take precedence over the times of impatience and doubt. The necessity for you to accept the truth that has been shared is very important. In the process you will become stronger, as we focus together to try yet another shift in consciousness. These shifts occur frequently, and though some may be subtle in nature, they are still necessary in order to continue this journey.

When my scribe asked me to shift time for her in order to ease the impact these morning session were having on her work day, I said, "You do it." For her this was an important lesson in the realization that she could create what she wanted in her life at any given moment. You must believe enough in what has been shared that when you are asked to create what you want, or to act in the state of being, you will *act*. For now, you are simply learning to come forth to embrace your own creative ability and take the steps that will lead to the big bang in creative force you seek. That is the way it is done in this third-dimensional reality where you presently reside. All I ask of you for now is that you begin to imagine that you can create what you want through focused intent and then come forth and create as if you have been doing it for lifetimes, for, in fact, you have.

Many of you may have experienced days or moments when time seemed to stand still, appeared to slow, or passed far too quickly. This is the shifting of time that can be experienced in this dimensional existence. Use your imagination and try this experiment if you will. Pick one moment in time and imagine it expanded to such an extent that you think it will never end, and then end it. Next, imagine you can speed up time and go from one experience to another in an instant. You may ask, "What happened just then? How is it that I was in one place in time and then, in an instant, found myself in another?" It is a mind game, to be sure, but one that can be used for the purpose of experiencing outside your limits. Shifting time has always been within your ability, but your awareness of such events stopped when you began letting the limit of the conscious mind replace the unconscious knowledge of this truth. While some of you are able to manipulate and experience this shifting of time, most have forgotten. Your creative life force will be waking up through this practice of shifting time. Many more abilities will begin to emerge from your contemplations and experiments in creation, simply by imagining it is so. With this enhanced awareness, you will begin to create a new way of projecting your thoughts without interference or doubt.

"Believe in the Self" is part of the equation that is most important and continually encouraged through these teachings. You shift time through the belief in the Self. The purpose is not only to move you from point A to point B but also to increase your awareness of all the little steps in between. It is in the conscious taking of these steps that wisdom is gained. It is a well known truth that each journey starts with one step. You have come forth into the act of being and into the belief in the Self in order to experience who you really are.

You possess two bodies—your earthbound body, which is subject to the gravitational pull of this planet, and your Soul or Spirit body which is aligned in totality with Original Thought. These bodies are combined to form your human life expressions displayed in a variety of colors, shapes and sizes. The Spirit body is made up of varying degrees and shades of pure energy unencumbered by limit. The Spirit body holds the memory of your connection to Original Thought and is your aeroship home. You may access your Spirit body more easily as you connect to Original Thought through prayer, meditation or in silent contemplation. A deeper relationship to your God is available to you during these quiet times of focus. When you pray or meditate, what do you ask for? Do you ask your God to spare you from suffering or fulfill your desires and bring you good fortune? Or do you empty your mind and ask your God to fill it up with the understanding of eternal truth? There is a distinct difference between the two. When you pray or meditate to ask for something, you are focused on an outcome from the limited-mind prospective. When you pray to open up your heart and to have it filled with the full knowledge and intent of Original Thought, you are focused on Spirit and the two separate bodies, the earthbound and Spirit body, become one.

When you are able to step out of conscious ego-mind long enough to allow Spirit to enter more fully, you have opened yourself to move out of body and into Spirit. This is an occasion for celebration, as it brings a balance between the human and Spirit that will cleanse the Soul. The body and Spirit will live as one, in full recognition and with greater success, when they are aligned. Each day, when I first begin to establish connection with my scribe for the purpose of recording the message, she experiences a feeling of heaviness in her body and the air around her begins to thicken. As the Spirit aligns more fully within her physical body and the True Mind is activated, we begin the transcriptions. What has been understood of the True Mind can also be said of the True Body, which is a united balance of Spirit and human existing as One. By walking the path of focused observation of the Self, and by your continued forward motion, you are gaining insight into your life and your true identity as an enlightened being. Your journey can be compared to that of the entire universal order, which is multi-layered, ever changing and continually growing and coming forth into the act of being. You are examining, perhaps for the first time, the many threads of unlimited thought creation that have been woven together with great care to produce the wonder of you. We will attempt to release the knots in these threads that keep you from merging completely with the full knowledge and truth of the Self.

In your prayerful contemplations, ask your Spirit to come forth and to balance more within the human body and walk with you in complete harmony as One. Your willingness and devotion to experiencing and living in full awareness in the act of being will bring the results you desire. And like a hunger within, you will begin to join forces once more with all that is true. Everything that is needed—everything you have ever been and will ever be—is fully contained within you. This knowing is alive in every atom of your body and in the insight gained through focused observation. Your potential for living and being in truth is endless. Wake up to the knowledge of what it is to be a whole, complete being on this planet, operating fully and simultaneously in a body as well as in Spirit. Contemplate this view from the window into your Soul, and embrace the opportunity to find perfect balance in truth.

Up to this point we have spoken of the beginning time and the first inhabitants on your planet. We have examined True Mind and True Body experience. I have presented an understanding of Original Thought and projected thought creation and how this knowledge relates to your life now. We have helped you unlock and examine the spaces in between your current reality and encouraged you to explore even further. You have been asked to conquer your fear and doubt and been presented with some outrageous material to digest in order to move you forward on your path to enlightened truth. What I am proposing is similar to a revolution that disrupts everything you believed to be true and makes you contemplate all possibilities. Some of you will be able to feel the shift and begin to mark this passing. Some will gain from the wisdom and move out into the world, tapping into their own guidance and serving in ways that will inform and uplift this planet into another more enlightened dimensional reality. At this time, part of your planet resides in the third dimension and part in the fourth dimension. Some layers even reside in the fifth and sixth dimensional realities. How can this be, when it appears you are still one planet revolving around the sun? Well, it is quite simple really, and is a truth found in the spaces in between.

Overlying this planet are higher frequencies and dimensions of reality that are available for you to experience at any given moment. There is knowledge to be gained in each dimension when one awakens and embraces higher wisdom such as this. These dimensions, filled with advanced knowledge and wisdom, can also be reached when you are in quiet contemplation and allow the unconscious mind to come forth and access the information that is readily available. Many of your great philosophers and inventors throughout the ages, when seeming to be in altered states of consciousness or asleep, were able to access information from this elevated state and bring it back to full expression in the third dimension. I believe the inventor of your light bulb, one Thomas Edison, often fell into these slumber-like states, out of which came some of his more revolutionary ideas. Some have been called crazy for what has been realized from these experiences, while others have been honored and gained great fame.

The Self is an aeroship that travels between these dimensional realities quite frequently and gains great wisdom in the process. This knowledge, though oftentimes unrealized, is held within your cellular memory until such time that you are ready to bring it forth. This is important to understand at this time, as many of you are being given the opportunity to access these higher truths when in the sleep state or in quiet contemplation, or when consciously seeking higher wisdom. When you come back into the third dimension from these experiences, you may feel as if you are walking in thick air—an apt description often used by my scribe. As your body begins to adjust and acclimate to these experiences, you will have a deeper understanding and motivation for what lies ahead; the waking mind will begin to access new insights and revelations more easily. This inter-dimensional travel is a process designed to peel away the many veils that separate you from the truth of the Spirit Body and help you to live more from within the True Body experience.

Living from within the True Body experience has not been accomplished by many in your Earth's history. Thousands of years ago, Jesus was able to travel quite easily between these dimensional realities. He brought the higher wisdom and energy of these realms to those who sought to gain knowledge from His teachings. While Jesus attempted to assist His followers to move with Him through the many layers of enlightenment and transcend all doubt, they gained only what they could from their limited perspective. For brief moments, some of His followers did transcend the third dimension to experience the wisdom He preached, but more often than not, their exposure to these insights were quickly forgotten with His passing, when Jesus left this third-dimensional existence and returned to the realm of Original Thought.

Throughout the ages, many great masters and teachers have come to move mankind closer to inter-dimensional awareness. Coming from limited thought perspective, the collective consciousness of the third dimension has effectively prevented many opportunities to advance this wisdom. Some of the exalted teachings of Jesus, the Buddha and other great and learned Masters have come and gone, leaving only traces of their greatness. In later years, the vast knowledge and subsequent teachings they brought were often altered to coincide with the present third-dimensional belief. As a result, some of the teachings and wisdom of these Masters became greatly diminished through limited interpretation.

Mankind is being prepared to expand third-dimensional understanding and embrace the wisdom of the ages. This revolution into the realm of all possibility and truth will not build another religion around it, nor a following, nor a shrine of any kind. Information will be passed along through the teachings of personal guides of the Spirit realm, master teachers in earthly form or on the written page. While in quiet contemplation and surrender to truth, you release the limits that have held you captive. My scribe has agreed to allow those of us who work with her to pass along such information through the written word. Her acceptance of this opportunity will open and elevate the Self, and she will become greater for the experience.

Remember this, mankind: *As you change and grow, all around will change and grow.* This is a consistent truth in your world, as well as in the whole of the universal order. With every step you take to embrace truth, you are reaching into and connecting more fully with higher dimensional realities, and the wisdom you gain will become integrated within your third- dimensional existence. Each dimensional shift brings you closer to the wisdom of the beginning time and that of Original Thought. Come forth into the act of being and believe in the Self until it simply becomes "being in truth." Through laughter, joy and a happy spirit, all will be accomplished. Awaken from your slumber and seize the opportunity to live a greater awareness through your open and giving heart.

## CHAPTER TWELVE

# EXPANDING TRUE MIND

*Mother took the occasion one morning to speak with me about our work together and the process of my evolution. It illustrates further many of the topics she had been teaching and life in general.*

In our short time together you have been given many insights and concepts to transcribe. You have listened with an open heart and recorded these pages of text as they were presented. Though the actual words may matter very little, listening to the spaces in between has helped you to discover the deeper truth of their meaning. Sometimes we sit in silence and no words come to fill the void. In the beginning, when Original Thought created form to inhabit the void, there were no words. You and I have created a bond through this silence.

In your daily practice with me you say a simple prayer to establish connection to the highest source and then wait to receive the message. Your intent is focused on recording accurately from the knowing of your True Mind connection to the truth. Though the printed words often seem too limiting to accurately convey the message as you understand it, they are all we have to work with at the moment. Some people will be reached through these words on the page, and others through the frequency vibration inherent in the way they are combined. What occurs for the reader who is willing to search is the opportunity to comprehend the truth waiting in between the lines of text.

What we accomplish together is the pursuit of all possibility and truth, and to live once more within the Original Thought of your creation. Will this make a change in your life? Most certainly. Will you have to move, change jobs or sit in an ashram for the rest of your life? No, no and no. The changes will be subtle at first, as you have already discovered. Little items may disappear and reappear, and you will barely take notice. You may briefly question what is happening but then go on about your day, relatively unaffected. This is how one lives on your planet. Everything around you is changing in structure, in consistency and in levels of awareness. You will begin to eat only those foods that nourish the body, have the ability to sustain a higher energy level throughout the day and may require less sleep. These changes and many more, will gradually unfold and be in accordance with the rhythm and timing of your evolution. I am speaking of what is to come in order to seed it in your conscious mind for later acceptance. You continue to listen between the lines of text and transcribe using words that are, at best, limited. I will continue to seed many outrageous things into your conscious mind and use the words that are presently available to do so. Your job is to record these words as given and then to keep moving forward. I plant the seeds and wait to see them come to fruition.

When the messages get caught up in your conscious mind's interpretation and you feel resistance to what is shared, your willingness to know what lies between the lines is very important. The words that the conscious mind seeks to edit are one thing and the truth that dwells between these lines, the deeper text, is quite another. The spaces in between are not open to interpretation but speak only the unfiltered truth. When you transcribe from this deeper message, you are working from the True Mind experience. Sometimes this knowing of the True Mind is realized more rapidly than the words on the page can be written and you feel unable to sustain the flow. When you are in this True Mind experience, it is like a state of *Samadhi*, or Oneness with the All. You have aptly described the physical experience to be much like walking through thick air. For now, these changes in conscious awareness will be subtle in order for the progression of the "act of being" to proceed.

Each day, upon arising, determine to be wholly present in your limited body and in the life that you have created. See your life for what it truly is—an illusion, a creation to fill the space until you no longer need it to progress. And dwell more in the space where truth and all possibility reside. I have spoken of the "spaces in between" extensively today because it is a concept that is solidifying within the unused portions of the temporal lobe, where true knowledge is stored.

When I first asked the question, "What do you want?" I desired your deeper understanding of Original Thought and the True Mind's potential. When you can answer that question from True Mind realization, then all things are possible. It is our purpose to teach you how to be ready to answer such a question as this. Until you can remember and know all that you possess in the uniqueness of True Body and True Mind, your ability to create will be limited. This capacity to create is one of the most precious gifts that you possess, but it also involves your commitment to integrity and accountability. A sense of responsibility and understanding of the Self must be fully present before you begin to create from the act of being. This is what it is all about.

You may feel that the ability to create should be easier and less complicated. In actuality, when you embrace a "state of being" more fully, it is easier. When you were told to create what you wanted in your life, you had some success. But it was never entirely what you wanted, or felt you wanted, at the time. Creating from the wisdom and place of being Original Thought, and from the True Mind experience, will help you achieve what you desire. When you have this awareness, you can determine what you want from a much deeper understanding and without outside interference.

For the purpose of aligning with the True Mind of Original Thought, we have gone back to where it all began and asked you to be more present from within the spaces in between the text. In the past you have been told that you could have this complete realization in an instant of recognition, and that continues to be true. But if you plant this belief into your present consciousness now, you may find your immediate desires unfulfilled. What I have asked you to do instead is pay attention to what is happening around you at any given moment. Be the observer, and the lessons you learn will bring you the truth that you seek. Do not become lost in the peaceful, solitary state of *Samadhi*, because that is not your purpose now. I would have you awake and aware at all times.

Your ability to create as a human entity involves much more than you have previously been led to believe. Creative force—your true life expression— is possible through the True Mind connection to Original Thought. When you are told to create your reality from this alignment, your consciousness begins to know that there is more to life than creating additional wealth, a better job or a love that is true, and you begin to see the bigger picture. There is always a bigger picture to be viewed if one only looks with eyes that do not see yet vision clearly. "Create your day" is not a new thought to be seeded in the conscious mind but a concept that has been presented by many teachers. What occurs from this understanding has the potential to benefit humankind beyond measure. We are providing only one piece of the puzzle of creation through True Mind connection, but it is an important one nonetheless.

There are many who have been touched by the realization of Original Thought, and they continually make themselves available to share in the cause of spiritual advancement. Some are more public than others. Their purpose, on a more global scale, is to stir this energy pot and assist humankind to move out of its third-dimensional mindset. Your job, through the transcription of these teachings, is to help clear the runway for more enlightened truth to be revealed. Through this effort, the cobwebs and dust bunnies of your mind will be removed to allow the True Mind to emerge at will.

There is a purpose in everything we do. There is an order to this world and to the journey of those who have been seeding your mind with similar information. It is analogous to the way in which Original Thought created in the beginning. New thought patterns are continually being formed, making inroads into your conscious awareness. Though this information may not feel new, it has awakened those portions of your brain that have lain dormant for eons. These insights are a wonderful gift called forth through the mantra *Come forth into the act of being and believe in the Self.* In an instant, you are capable of realizing everything that you have been from the beginning and everything you will ever be. There are instantaneous realizations when coming forth into the act of being.

You are awakening, and when given this opportunity, you seek and will find what is true.

You have been shown the truth but have yet to fully cognize it. It is a challenging process. Throughout our time together, you will begin to expand your True Mind through new experiences. During these times you may feel drowsy or out of sync with your world, but this will pass as these experiences create inroads into your brain. The words that are transcribed each day on these pages are inadequate to describe what truly occurs each time we sit together like this. Continue to Believe in the Self, the Self first birthed from Original Thought, and that will make all the difference.

We will close for today as you greet another dawn. This is a metaphor for all you have been given. There is always another dawn and another clean slate to be written on and lessons to be observed and lived. Each day your slate is washed clean then comes forth into the act of being anew. What a wonderful opportunity to consciously go forth into the dawn of all possibilities. Greet your day, for it is a wonderful gift that is given unto you—one you have created. Now be at peace within your brilliance.

CHAPTER THIRTEEN

# THE SINGLE CELL

*All life in a single cell. The entire universe contained in one solitary atom.* I speak to you now mankind; everything that you have ever been, or ever will be, is contained in this one tiny unit of life. It is a truth that may seem preposterous, yet at the same time most wonderful to conceive. And it is absolutely accurate. This is your life force as created by Original Thought. When you first began to contemplate the vastness and complexity of the universal order, its grandeur may have been difficult to imagine. Yet here you are, all life contained in a single unit of being. How can you be this seed that grew such brilliance? From a single cell stars were created. Because of you, lava flowed to form and shape the landscape, while the sun appeared to crest the mountain tops. You have controlled your destiny, molded kingdoms, created great beauty and allowed everything, for the adventure. All life sparked from this tiny origin of being, this single cell. You.

Mankind has been virtually unaware of the truth of its creative potential for far too long, but that is beginning to change. This little planet of yours is being constantly bombarded with waves of energy and truth that will light your journey's path. There will be those who embrace this information and are compelled to bring it to the world, while others will sit in quiet contemplation, integrate the knowledge and live it in awareness. One is not greater than the other, but each one follows its truth.

When I sat with my scribe this morning, her mind was occupied with fleeting thoughts and plans for the day. Her conscious mind was fully engaged with incessant chatter, not allowing access to the unconscious mind's wisdom and insight. Some of you have been taught to meditate and set aside the conscious mind in order to more easily access the unconscious. This is a very good practice to continue, but the ultimate goal is to combine the two into what we call the "one True Mind experience." Before my scribe begins to record the daily message, she connects to the subconscious, or spirit-mind. The chatter from the conscious mind begins to fade and the complete merging of the two into one mind is complete. It is then, within this True Mind experience, that the messages are recorded without interference.

Those of you who have come here to live and grow and adventure on this planet have forgotten much of your creative potential. To guard against the truth of who you are, conscious ego-mind was born. It is going to be awhile yet before we completely dig you out of this one, but some of you are committed to doing just that. In the process, you will gain an understanding of the True Mind and of the adventure called "the Self." You are not operating in the caves of the Himalayas any longer but instead in the caves of the mind. I am attempting to bring the Light into the shadows of fruitless thought patterns so you may begin to change them and gain from the experience. It is how you learn. You have a thought, you contemplate it, and you question and seek the truth and then act on it. Truth may be given to you when you least expect it. It is why I have cautioned you to be the observer of your life and to pay attention to everything. It is during these times of observation and contemplation that you are in perfect alignment with wisdom and truth.

When I ask you to accept that the All is contained in the smallest unit of life, you can begin to see my meaning. The answers to your questions and yearnings, the intangibles you fear are out of reach, are contained within each tiny atom and cell of your body. You are the creator and the creation, the complete answer from the beginning of the thought of you in the mind of God. You have always had the answers. This truth is as lofty as one may wish to make it, or as simple. Contemplate the atom, the human cell. Do some scientific research on what is known by today's scientists. Read of great Masters and what they taught. Read what Jesus said that is written in your ancient Bible. Look between the lines of information and contemplate the meaning through your new perspective as the observer. Do some research.

Your conscious ego mind often acts as a filter to the truth of your creative potential and Oneness. The conscious mind considers itself a protector of your human existence. Historically, many of your greatest teachers and philosophers have been persecuted and condemned by those who feared the expansion of Spirit. Any attempt to expand this ego consciousness was, and continues to be, greatly judged. Ridicule is the sport of a limited mind, and some individuals feel safer operating from this restricted perspective. I am not here to speak to those who accept limits, although everything is allowed. The events leading to the discovery of truth for each individual is controlled by their human intent. From our perspective, it is a common occurrence to watch the awakening Spirit of some while continuing to allow the limits of others. For those who remain in limit, the truth of their existence will be realized in their own timing. What is spoken by the many Masters who have come before you is the truth that some of you seek. These Masters are not greater than you but are fully awakened. They have achieved, through the expansion of their conscious mind, the ability to merge more within the Spirit and the one True Mind. Great Masters have often walked this earth and operated solely within True Mind. Once True Mind is fully achieved, it is never abandoned. Once attained, True Mind awakens one from the dream, and you are reunited within the realm of the single atom, the universal cell and Original Thought.

Contemplate what has been shared and take note of when, in your busy day, you are able to slip the boundaries of the conscious mind and live more within True Mind. When the Spirit comes upon you, there will be a peacefulness that transcends human limit, and in that moment you become the realized Self. This pause in your day may be as brief as the beating of a butterfly's wing but will register in your conscious mind and cannot be denied. You have opened the door to the exploration of truth and must continue to move through it in order to experience the other side. It is an adventure you control. Do not be fearful. What has opened for you is the realm of all possibility, and you will reap rewards beyond imagining.

*When Mother spoke of that moment in time when you become the realized Self, it reminded me of an experience I once had walking along the beach on a blustery*

*winter's day. The wind was strong, as the waves crashed to the shore with great force. About halfway up the beach, with a heavy heart and thoroughly into my moody musings, I stopped. As I slowly turned toward the sea, I began to feel a sudden and peculiar stillness surrounding me. The waves still crashed to shore, but I couldn't hear them. The wind was silent, but neither sound nor movement entered into my space. Was this how it felt to be in the eye of a storm? In this stillness I felt an incredible peace and contentment. I stood there in the silence, taking in the beauty and the tranquility of the moment, and I thanked God for being present with me that day. And as quickly as the silence had come, it moved on and I resumed my walk in the wind. I asked Mother about this later and shared my feeling that I had been in the eye of a storm, and she replied:*

> "Yes, exactly so. There was almost a stilling of time, an opening in the eye of God to go right to the heart, right to the core of what is needed. You could sense in that vibration of stillness that that which is called "time" is beginning to collapse on humanity, but not in a negative way. So there you were protected, and there you were able to see on some level of your being a great freedom from all your strife, which is only an illusion."

*I said that I felt alone there on the beach, but not lonely.*

> "Indeed, for you were with the Self, and the Divine realization of truth is coming into place there."

You have come to a crossroads in your journey. Will you continue to seek your truth, or will you stay with what is familiar? Will you stay in your box of human limits, or step out for an adventure? You are the only one who can answer these questions. Begin to walk through each day with heightened awareness. Listen to the sounds. Touch, taste and feel your life. Contemplate the opportunity that your senses give you to acknowledge what you know of your human existence. Observe your day and everything that surrounds you; fully experience what you have created. There is nothing fixed about your creation. In an instant of awareness you can change anything from a solid state into something altogether different. Creation is liquid, not static. It is enough to contemplate for now. I am here to poke holes in your dream and let the light shine through—the light of truth, fully contained in the tiniest atom within every cell.

When coming forth into the act of being, those of us who inhabited this planet in the days of its birth knew exactly what that meant. We created from this place of certainty. Our creations bore fruit and multiplied. It was a time of unending adventure and great learning. We learned that when one is able to exist from this place of *being* and live in truth, a light more brilliant than the sun is present to show the way. When one walks away from this path and makes choices that cause harm or inhibits the growth of another in any way, the light is dimmed and darkness descends. This realization is best illustrated by the symbol of the yin and yang. These curved half-circles of light and dark fit together as one. Within each half-circle, located in the center, is an opposing colored sphere, which serves to illustrate that in all light there is darkness and in all darkness there is light. In the many and varied kingdoms of Original Thought there are always opposites to be considered, and you have the free will and the opportunity in every journey taken to select what serves the greater good.

I have spoken of the Self and the journey traveled for each individual soul, each spark of creation. Now I will speak to you of the "collective consciousness," which is important to recognize at this time. When we speak of the "greater good," we are creating a picture in the conscious mind of our responsibility toward all humanity. Further expand this view of the greater good to encompass All That Is—all creation, even the smallest leaf. Now look upon your beautiful planet and use this vision to move out and include the vastness of the void and all that dwells within it. Experience the life force within the universal order and know that the greater good encompasses it all. What can you do to bring about more light to all of creation? First realize that no single thought or action is truly isolated. These thoughts move out into your world and beyond to reverberate and create a multitude of reactions through time and space. What is being created at any given moment is the collective thought of like-minds with similar direction and purpose. Those of us who reside in a reality other than your third dimensional one possess the ability to see clearly beyond limitations. The dimensional realities of the universal order are vastly more numerous than you can imagine. The void and all the spaces in between have no limit. The void is never static but continually grows and expands.

It is important to understand completely that what may seem insignificant to you is also included in what is called "the greater good." Each time something or someone on your planet dies or is injured from lack of care, through violence or because of pollution or neglect, it is a reflection on the greater good and influences every corner of the universal order. When the darkness is allowed to grow without the light, the negative effect is multiplied many times. Thus begins a path of destruction that is difficult to stop. That is why the circle of light is included within the darkest part of the yin and yang symbol. This circle of light is never static but bubbles with energy and potential as an influence within that darkness. This light pulses with the energy of the greater good and serves as a reminder to those who would dwell only in the dark thoughts of their creations that there is another way.

In the history of all cultures, religious beliefs and shared stories of old, there are numerous tales that illustrate good, triumph over evil. I ask you to make a commitment to the Light, even though you may feel you've already done so. It is a commitment that must be made continually in order to grow and become greater still. Your commitment to the Light and to the greater good involves awareness, observation and the act of being. It means that you must pay attention to everything and know that the greater good is found in all existence throughout the universal order. Pay attention to the darkness when it comes into your thoughts, your speech or your vision. Pay attention and be ever vigilant, for you must choose the Light consciously in every moment. In so choosing, you allow the darkness to recede and become dormant. In the symbol of the curved, half-circle of light, the dark area appears as a static sphere waiting only for the focus of your life force to bring it to life. Now do you begin to understand? When one focuses on the darkness in even the most insignificant way, one imbues it with life force and gives it the potential to become more than it was ever intended to be. Make your focus the greater good at all times.

Continue to be vigilant and observe where you place your focus each moment of the day. Words spoken or actions performed in anger or hate bring the darkness into focus. Do you choose to focus your life force within the dark circle or within the light that surrounds it? You must choose in every moment. It is through this action that your journey will continue in the light of all truth.

# CHAPTER FOURTEEN

# THE SOUL COMPUTER

Deep in the soul of mankind there is a seed, a kernel, not yet ready to sprout. This seed is the future time, the harbinger of things to come. This seed will bring forth fruit that is unbearably sweet and ripe and full. This seed holds the memory of the beginning and the spaces in between. You, mankind, are the awakening Spirit, the Soul essence that springs forth upon a new day. You have been taken back to the beginning and brought forward with great care to glimpse the future and hold the vision of what you are yet unable to see. You have been given these truths, and they have been absorbed into the essence of your Soul.

When I call upon you to feel that expansion of the Soul—to recognize and accept that the kernel of truth is upon you—I do so to enable you to wear the cloak of timelessness. You have been taught by many Masters, and some very important and far-reaching scientists of the day, that all time co-exists—that everything is happening simultaneously and there is no separation of past, present and future; there is only now. When I ask you to remember the past and look toward the future, it is only to placate that part of your conscious ego mind that will not allow this expanded insight of spirit-mind.

We speak of the Soul today because the Soul remembers everything. It is the life force that is your own personal spark of Original Thought. The Soul lives on when the human body dies. The Soul is eternal and has recorded and retained everything from the inception of Original Thought. The Soul remembers it all. When I sit with my scribe, communicating through words on a page, her Soul memories surface and take precedence over the limits of her conscious mind. Each time she focuses thusly she is experiencing her own personal revelation. As the sun is bid to light the day each dawn, her Soul memory awakens and the truth is written. This is a quiet time between us, undisturbed by outside influences and chatter, and during this finite space of time, we are in accord. When you read these words and then go forth unto your day, you carry this truth, this experience, with you and are changed forever. You may not appear different to the outside world, but inside your Soul a revolution is beginning to take hold.

The Soul has the ability, though still attached by an ethereal cord, to leave your human body to journey. Usually this occurs when you drop off to sleep or "space out," as I have heard it called. The Soul can leave the body and in a split second of timelessness return without you being any the wiser. And what is the purpose of the Soul's journey? As you begin to open and allow a shift in consciousness, the Soul expands and pulsates to a frequency vibrational force that is magnetically drawn toward higher dimensions. The Soul gravitates toward higher vibrational force, gains from the knowledge and integrates it within the human conscious mind as truth, and everything is changed forever. The separation of time does not exist. There is no past or future; there is only now. And through these experiences and insights into coexisting time, the conscious, ego mind will be able to accept the truth. We can only speak to where you are now from your limited perspective, not necessarily to what is true in totality.

While the Soul journeys and is attracted to vibrational frequencies of other dimensions, the body remains here in gravitational, earthbound awareness. You don't always remember these shifts of consciousness, but you will know of your Soul's journey through the subtle ways in which you begin to change. In any given situation, you might say to yourself, *This used to bother me, but it doesn't anymore.* From the Soul's journey, you have integrated greater wisdom from a higher source and expanded truth into a specific experience. It can happen in an instant. Acknowledge and accept these occurrences as realizations of positive growth and change and times of great expansion.

Your Soul yearns to be united with the Source in full recognition. Your Soul is separated from what has birthed it, much like a baby is brought forth from the womb of its mother. While in the womb, the baby feels no limit and is complete and whole within the comfort of the fluid that sustains and cradles it. The baby breathes in unison with its mother— one pulse, one heartbeat in complete accord. Did you know that the Soul of the baby comes and goes? The Soul, which is Original Thought, experiences growth and development while living within the womb and also comes and goes at will during this time. The commitment of some Souls to live in the human body is often not made until the birth is complete and life has been sustained outside the womb for many weeks, and sometimes months, of its existence. The Soul comes and goes in the newborn until such time as it commits to stay or decides to leave the body through what is termed "death." When the final decision is made to stay housed within the human existence and to experience what has come to be known as "life" on this planet, the Soul stays put, for the most part.

So, now you have a committed Soul housed in the form of a baby, ready to take on the world and what it has come forth to experience. In the first few years of life—some ten of your years—a Soul will have cause to remember, in dreams and flashes of insight, what lies beyond the limited human body. Up until the tenth year, many children may speak truths that seem incomprehensible to the adults in their immediate environment. These truths are accessed occasionally in the dream state and then, upon awakening, quickly forgotten. As children grow and mature, they soon learn to suppress what they know and understand as unique sparks from Original Thought. These forgotten memories are always retained in the unconscious mind or Spirit consciousness, for they are part of the Soul's origin. The Soul's memory is available to you whenever you so desire, but when these memories are repressed, you find your life firmly entrenched in ego-mind consciousness. Though the ability to access the Spirit consciousness is found in the dream state, upon waking, these experiences are most often forgotten, and life continues much as it did before. *The Soul lives and never dies* is a powerful truth. The Soul never dies, and what it knows is always available to you, should you wish to become a seeker of truth. When you desire to know your origin, your true beginning, then the yearning of the Soul sets you on the path that will lead you home. Through focused intent and your acknowledgment of the Self as the spark from Original Thought, you reap the rewards of all possibility and truth.

"Come forth into the act of being and believe in the Self" is your link to the Soul and true Spirit of your existence.

Though similar in many ways, each Soul is unique and the vibrational pulse that leads you home to true enlightenment. The Soul is your body as One, your True Mind, your Original Thought and your ultimate completion, though certainly not the end. Quite the opposite. The Soul is the perpetual beginning and like the void, it is also ever-expanding and changing, growing and completely alive. Original Thought is never static but pulses with life force. You have the opportunity to reconnect and fully embrace this realization, though in truth you have never been disconnected.

The infinite numbers of Souls who reside on your planet have various lifestyles and experiences. In this melting pot of humanity that bubbles with vitality and Soul essence, there exists beauty and light as well as darkness and pain. Throughout time, communication has been nurtured between Spirit beings and the humans on this planet. How these experiences have manifested depended upon the individual cultures and their beliefs. Some Spirit beings have appeared as angels and others as religious deities. Some have taken on the guise of a masterful teacher and assembled great followings, while others have sat quietly and listened to words of truth and transcribed them onto the page. How enlightenment and change is presented depends entirely upon the culture in which the human lives. The wisdom of the spirit-mind has always been available to those who acknowledge the Soul in truth and the power of Original Thought. When one comes forth into the act of being and believes in the Self and is more connected to truth, they cannot stay hidden from this reality any longer.

And the Soul yearns. It yearns to bring forth what it has never forgotten. It yearns to clear the cobwebs from limited consciousness and uncover the truth that lies within the spirit-mind. The Soul yearns to return to the True Mind housed in the True Body of mankind and be as One with Original Thought once more. When humans pass into what you call "death," they view their life and the people they have left behind as if through a thin veil. For the most part, they understand they can no longer be viewed as a life form and may be drawn to stay with what is familiar. They have yet to hear the voice that is calling them back to Original

Thought realization and continue to haunt their former life, unable to interact with those who remain. For some, it is impossible to move beyond this veil. They never heed that voice calling them to come forth into the light of Original Thought connection. They are called "ghosts" or "apparitions", viewed briefly by some but never truly seen, for they are beyond the veil of earthbound existence. The voice that is calling them home will never rest until they turn once more toward the light of true awakening. This awakening is the Soul's yearning to connect completely to Original Thought realization, and a time of great joy. When I speak of *coming home*, I do not speak of what has been called "eternal rest." What would be the purpose for wanting to sleep or rest for all eternity? The Soul is eternal and lives to explore and expand. The Soul is never static and moves in and out of the void in a never-ending cycle of rebirth. Think of Original Thought as an equal opportunity employer. Anyone can join the firm of enlightened Soul essence; anyone and everyone. There are unlimited opportunities for growth. The only thing that may hold you back is your judgment of what you have experienced. What limits do those judgments place upon your growth in Spirit? View these judgments honestly and you will discover there are truly no restrictions where Soul experience is concerned. Everything is possible and your body doesn't have to die to further the journey. Do not waste your time feeling frustrated or impatient for these revelations to come to fruition. Take these kernels of knowledge and, through careful nurturing, watch them grow into the truth of who you are. You are One with the eternal Light, the Soul essence of Original Thought. Feed this spark of desire to know, and Come forth into the act of being and believe in the Self. Now you have a better understanding of what that Self represents. It is a good beginning.

I would like you to picture your Soul as a distinctive, life force-driven aeroship. Your life force is what sees you through the maze of experiences that you encounter in human form. While life force can be diminished, expanded or manipulated in the human, the Soul cannot. The Soul is unique, whole and perfect in every aspect. The Spirit-Soul is not just human experience or emotion but your own unique spark of Original Thought. The Soul is pulsing, vibrant and complete. The Soul has the ability to journey throughout an infinite number of dimensional realities at the same time, for the opportunity to learn and expand.

You are the sparks from Original Thought and not confined to a single dimensional existence. What you are presently experiencing in human form is but a fraction of the opportunities that abound. As a multi-dimensional, experiential being you may choose to center your attention or expression in only one dimension at a time. At this moment, you are focused on the pages in this book. For just one moment, try to imagine a dimensional reality where one doesn't have to scribe on paper but can register all that is known on a "Soul computer" that travels with you wherever you go. Imagine moving in and out of multidimensional realities with your Soul aeroship carrying complete information from the beginning of time and all the spaces in between, even before those spaces existed. It can boggle the mind, or set it free. But this is the truth of who you are. When you begin to experience and contemplate this kind of expansive information, you may be overwhelmed and may understand why this concept of multiple realities is not discussed more. It would be rather like force-feeding a baby intricate mathematical equations and expecting it to fully comprehend. You have chosen to limit such information in order to live and operate as a human on this planet. Your planet is beautiful, and the opportunities for growth are as abundant and unique as those of you who have come to have these experiences. But I have another purpose for those willing to listen. If you believe you are truly this unique Soul, this spark from Original Thought, then it must follow that you are also unlimited. How could it be any other way? As a unique, unlimited Soul, you have many choices, and making these choices can and does change your limited perspective. You have chosen to journey on a planet of limited spiritual and sensory experience. Yet, within these agreed-upon limitations, you have continued to produce wonders that are like a beacon to many in the void. When I speak of the void as being liquid and ever-expanding, you must rid yourself of the dictionary version of what "void" means. In reality, the void is a place of all possibility and truth, ever changing and expanding with life force. In one way or another, every interaction you have in any dimensional reality has an effect on them all. The aeroship called the Spirit-Soul moves you in and out of these dimensional realities. Your Soul retains the memory of each encounter and, as your own personal computer, registers every experience and organizes every thought. This Soul computer allows you to focus and function completely in whatever dimensional existence you wish to experience. The Soul never dies, never forgets and is ever expanding, learning and growing.

A reasonable facsimile of one aspect of the Soul computer has been produced in your Star Trek movies, where one simply speaks into a computer the food it wishes to produce and the food appears. Thought is spoken and a product is manifested. The inspiration for this creation happened when the writers accessed the knowledge existing and available in another dimensional reality. This is but one example of the ideas and concepts created and integrated into current experience from the Spirit-Soul's inter-dimensional travel. The Soul, as your aeroship can and does provide you with opportunities that are vastly unique and never-ending.

A few learned teachers and spiritual Masters have come to speak to those who are prepared to listen and move beyond earthly limits. Once fully awakened, some of these Masters no longer wish to live within the confines of limit and choose to move beyond this third-dimensional existence. The humans who remain in denial of the bigger picture and don't believe in life everlasting might end the life of their bodies and go into a very deep sleep until they are ready to wake into the Light. Each person is unique, and the experiences they choose create many opportunities for growth.

This is what I ask of you: Quiet the mind, so you may come to hear and know the whispered messages of your Soul. Just for this one moment in time, accept the possibility that you are traveling and operating within multiple dimensions and experiences simultaneously. Your Soul is your etheric computer and keeps everything organized and operating smoothly. The only virus that can infect this Soul computer is *doubt*. Accept what has been given and registered in the conscious mind and live each day as you have before, if you can. You are more awake now than you realize and will not slumber within limits much longer. Allow your Spirit-Soul to operate as intended. Stop and listen occasionally to your Soul, and embrace these moments of peace that open doors, revive old memories and then program the new data you have received.

Contemplate the Star Trek computers that quickly manifest what desire has been spoken into them. This is a computer worth having, is it not? Consider the possibility of creating what you want at any given moment with a single thought or spoken word. When you begin to move beyond the restriction of limited thought, you become mindful of your inherent ability to create at will. This realization carries with it a responsibility on your part to explore the Self more fully. When you arrive at that point in your evolution, you will see that what you wish to create won't be more gold or true love or perpetual youth and beauty. What you will manifest from this unlimited knowledge will be much more expansive.

Be patient on this journey. Be patient and accept that you are on a quest to go beyond the limited thought projections of the human mind and expand your life force. It is just a beginning. It is always and forever a beginning. There is no end to what will be accomplished. If you are to continually expand and grow, then you are always at the beginning of your journey. You may see your path as having a beginning, middle and an end, but there is truly never an end. There will, however, be moments in time when you may place your focus in one dimension or another in order to adjust to this new expansion. This is what you call "living your life." While you are in this place called "life," this contemplative state of being, your Soul experiences continue. You draw those life lessons designed to wake you from slumber and get you moving. Some experiences may be painful but may also be a great motivator to awaken. When you stop doubting that there is more than this limited existence, you begin to eliminate painful experiences from your life. Your life becomes simpler as the slate is swept clean. During this period of cleansing and releasing what does not serve you, feelings of pain and loss may grip you so tightly that you are unwilling to take another step. Give yourself the time to grieve this loss of what has been until you can recognize it for what it is and then be ready to journey again. This is often the time of greatest growth and change.

Ask for guidance, and you will find those who await your calling with beneficial insight and ready assistance. Listen to those who bring you support. Soon you will be able to continue, and the past will become a mere blip on your screen as your life force expands. There is only the Self on the Soul journey of expansion. You will see, for you have called it forth. Now grab hold with both hands and follow my lead for yet awhile until you are completely awake and can see me for what I am—your reflection.

# CHAPTER FIFTEEN

# THE TRUE MIND EXPERIENCE

Wrapped tightly in the womb of forgetfulness, mankind has been in a dream state for eons, never once sparking the least bit of interest to wake up and be birthed into a new awareness. It's time you woke up!

The first pioneers on planet earth came for the adventure and the opportunity to learn and gain from the experience called the "emerging planet." Using creative, projected thoughts, they populated the planet and made agreements as to the feasibility and longevity of each creation. To maintain a balance of all that was created throughout the lands and monitor the many groups populating the remote areas of your world, a universal council of elders was formed. In time, some of these pioneers began to slumber in a state of forgetfulness and to experience their lives as limited beings. It was through this loss of unlimited perception and God awareness that the unraveling of the adventure began. And mankind became trapped in the womb of forgetfulness.

Often when the conscious ego mind is given information that it is unable or unwilling to accept, it begins to shut down. The opening into your box of limited perception starts to close and you lose the ability to connect to the True Mind experience. When my scribe experiences such resistance, yet continues to push through her perceived limits, the brain's temporal lobe is activated. The process of stepping out of limited consciousness—expanding and merging with the subconscious mind—promotes a balance between the two, and that becomes the one True Mind experience.

The True Mind experience can be accessed readily within the awakened human when he ceases to slumber and begins to gain insights into other realms of possibility and truth. When True Mind is fully operational, you will feel the difference. During this process, however, there may be times when you find it difficult to navigate as before in your present reality. You would do well to take your time and integrate this state of being into your life gradually. Sit quietly with focused breath and allow this transition to resonate within you. Do not force what you think is expected. This is a part of the journey for those who seek to be truly awake. Like your fabled Rip Van Winkle, you will awaken and realize that everything has changed when, in reality, nothing has changed. Your reality is simply being viewed from another higher perspective.

Throughout history there have been individuals who have experienced such awakenings. They have envisioned kingdoms beyond belief, written texts of learning, shared their insights and traveled to the stars and back. These visionaries have helped make it possible for humankind to realize that their opportunities are endless and truly without limit. You must seek your peace in truth, wherever you may find it. The Buddha sat under that tree for a very long time in his process of awakening. And you are attempting to do this within the parameters of your busy, human life. Be kind and patient with yourself, and begin your awakening with ease. Never force what cannot be rushed, for the timing of your evolution is important.

If you are willing to allow these shifts of consciousness, you can expect to be kept off balance. That is what a shift must do. You must be thrown out of your comfort zone and given a push toward Spirit-Soul memory in order to progress. Once you are committed to these changes, you must get through the process as best you can. If you need to sit in meditation, do so. If the words on these pages make no sense to you, take the time to rest and sit under the Buddha tree and just be with the Self. The only expectations are ones you put on yourself. This process is totally motivated and guided by the One who has never forgotten and is your own best teacher, the eternal Self. There is no way to make a mistake, for you are that spark from Original Thought. Take the time to reach a little deeper and embrace your truth and be at peace. Listen to that still small voice within. We are here to help and guide you. You are never alone.

The acceptance of the one True Mind consciousness allows a shift in how you view the world. Events in your life that have prevented growth and delayed happiness and out-of-the-box thinking are eliminated. You have heard it said you are the creator of everything that occurs in your life, and this is true to a certain extent. In the caves of learning, one of the most important things we discovered was the influence that group consciousness had on our projected thoughts and how it could compromise our creative intent if not used for purposeful good in full cooperation. In order for you to truly create without interference, you must exist and operate fully from within the one True Mind. True Mind is a well-run, intricately-operated flow of energy vibration. How do you recognize when True Mind is in operation? You wake up one morning and notice that all around you has changed. The sun is brighter and your mind sharper. You smile more and cry less. Operating from the True Mind, you access your knowing Spirit and embrace what you have previously been denying, and are richer for it. Take this time for a closer look at your life as you begin to live more fully out of the box of limits.

Mankind, you have been much like a sleepwalker who goes about his day performing tasks that are endless in order to perpetuate your life. You have been asleep for a very long time. How does it feel to finally begin to awaken? There is nothing written that says you have to sleepwalk through your life. Only in your world, with this continued belief in separate minds, does this sleepwalking habit persist. When you begin to live your journey out of the box, you are less interested in the old ways of thinking. When you desire change—not just the promise of change—you embrace this awakened state of consciousness. In this state of awareness, new goals have replaced the ones you had in the waking slumber you called "your life." I speak of "slumber" as the place of separate minds, and "awakening" as the state of True Mind. For a while yet, you will move between slumber and wakening as you shed the one and begin operating more fully within the other. Pay attention to your experiences throughout each day; they will give insights as to the differences between them. These experiences become opportunities that enable the shift into True Mind consciousness to begin.

The integration of the conscious and the unconscious mind into one True Mind is much like the weaving of a cloth. The end result is a rich tapestry of color, potential and life force. Examine your thought patterns and ask yourself, *What if?* *What if,* instead of accepting that time moves forward at a structured pace, you believe you can slow it down or speed it up as you wish? *What if,* instead of believing that pain must accompany a life experience, you believe that pain does not exist? *What if* you alter your beliefs and create only joy and peace in your life? When you choose to exist in this state of creation for even a short period of time, you are living in the presence of True Mind consciousness.

At present, your conscious mind accepts what it has determined to be "fixed absolutes" in life. When you take an absolute—a mindset or a belief—and turn it around so that it serves your desire and intent in any given situation, you have begun to achieve True Mind existence. I say "begun to achieve" because it takes effort and commitment on your part to make the shift. The first step is to be mindful of your thoughts and beliefs. You must determine the absolutes that exist in your world. Keep the ones that serve you and change the ones that don't. You must become mindful and observe everything. Take your time, for it probably won't happen in an instant. Let's take a look at the absolute operating in this previous statement. A specific belief of the conscious ego mind has been perfectly illustrated for you. "It probably won't happen in an instant" is an absolute that plants the seed of doubt and can prevent forward movement. Use this opportunity to spark the memory of a time when you could change everything and anything in an instant of desire. You will be bringing that ability back through True Mind consciousness once again. Make this your new absolute for the future.

Begin today to practice mindfulness as it relates to your personal absolutes. You are in the process of clearing out the cobwebs of your conscious mind and must first learn to walk before you are released to run. I caution you to take these steps carefully. I do not want you to feel you have failed while attempting to achieve something that you may not be ready to do as yet. I am taking you carefully, step by step, and laying the groundwork for further expansion. There is no failure to be experienced, no hesitation and no reluctance as we take these steps together. Taking these steps is one absolute we will use until it is no longer necessary. Go about your day and pay attention to the absolutes that surround you and are woven into the fabric of your life. Do not judge them, but simply be the observer for now. This is how you learn and prepare the way for future explorations into True Mind awareness. It is truly an adventure worth exploring.

# CHAPTER SIXTEEN

# THE SOUL BRAIN

In order for focused thought to be fully realized, the temporal lobe must be activated. When awakened, access to the known brain, as well as those areas of the brain that have yet to be discovered, will be possible. When mankind begins to access these unused portions, the ability to utilize deeper brain function will be possible.

In the beginning, when your world was populated by those of us from beyond this universe, the human bodies we created were much taller than the humans of today and equipped with a fully functional brain. Our brains were able to compute data, create from focused thought and cognize information gathered from experience at an accelerated rate. These were only a few of our capabilities then and are really only a few of what you possess now. Your brain is of a similar design and is as proficient as ours. Through the millions of years and vast experiences lived on planet earth, you have lost and gained many of the innate abilities of the brain.

While the brain and the body were intended to work together in harmony, it is obvious from your history of disease that your current functioning brain is often counter-productive to the whole. Your brain, in present form, is fully capable of enlightenment. You may ask if that is true, why is mankind not enlightened? It is a very good question. The answer will help you integrate this truth into the temporal lobe and align it within the higher portions of your reasoning Soul brain.

The scientists of today have speculated that humans use only about 10% of the brain's current ability. They are basically correct, but it is a rather high estimate on their part. You actually utilize as little as 2%. Yet, even from this minute portion of the brain in use, you have accomplished many things, and this is a very important distinction to understand. Just as there are several overlays and dimensional layers to your world, so is the brain many-layered and able to operate independently in several dimensional realities at once. Presently, your human brain is operating in a reality that keeps conscious awareness limited to the senses of touch, smell, taste, vision and hearing. The Soul brain houses the subconscious insights that help assist the expansion of more esoteric ideas and total connection to the God Self. This is what is meant when I speak of the "abilities" of the Soul brain and the human temporal lobe. The connection and inter-relatedness of these layers—or dimensions—of brain function are dependent upon the fully awakened temporal lobe. This particular part of the human brain is the bridge that will begin to expand and blend the human and Soul brain together into one functioning unit.

Do you see a pattern beginning to emerge here? First, we spoke of your two minds, and you were told that you would be combining them into one True Mind. Then we spoke of the bodies and combining them into one True Body. Now we speak of the various dimensions and overlays of the brain and talk of combining the current human brain and the Soul brain into one complete and functional motor to drive your human vehicle. You are being encouraged to bring more of the dimensional layers of the Self into harmony and build bridges between the seeming opposites that are operating now. Contemplate this seed being planted and let it germinate. At times, the information that is shared may seem incomplete and confusing. It is presented in this way, step by step, to enhance your understanding and facilitate further growth. I am from the time before your beginning, and some information that will be given has not been shared like this before. Cognizing such information, in the only area of the brain that will allow the bridge between the two brains to be ignited, is the purpose. The words on these pages do not begin to describe the intricacies and the power of your thoughts that allow the opening structures to be built.

Take a moment to sit with this information and begin to assimilate this Original Thought pattern into the temporal lobe of your brain. Focus on drawing imaginary lines from the tops of both ears and forward toward the center top of the eye sockets. Continue this line upward and around to the back of the head and down toward each side of the bottom portion of the occipital bone located at the base of your skull and then back across to the openings of each ear. Draw these imaginary, circular lines around the entire area on both sides of your head. This temporal lobe area is much larger than has been previously identified. It is not completely made of brain matter but is split between matter and a dimensional layer of understanding that involves sound vibration that cannot be seen or felt with the human sensory system. The connections to the ear canal, and to the inner workings that allow you to use your auditory sense, are located here and allow the bridge to be connected between the two brains. It is in this area of temporal lobe focus where dimensional layers exist and are more easily accessed. We planned well in the beginning, reveling in our creative ability. We planned well, indeed, for we could see this time coming and we prepared for it. So for now, just accept that you will have those occasions when the combining of the two brains, through the bridge of the temporal lobe experience, will be more accessible.

There is great significance in labeling the "Soul brain" as such. The Soul is an etheric idea that is impossible to see or experience in your waking state. Some wonder if it even exists. Others believe that when you die, your Soul carries you beyond human existence and lives forever in heaven. The Soul brain represents just such an idea, beyond human experience or understanding. More importantly, what I would like you to consider is the concept of the human as a "whole Being." You are not a creation that needs separate yet functioning parts to make it whole. You are completely whole from inception. Radical? Blasphemous? Probably, and, most likely for some of you, a concept that is as difficult to wrap your mind around as the concept of the Soul as being separate from, yet a part of, you.

Contemplate for a moment that humankind is, in reality, a Soul-less being. What doubts come forth instantly from this statement? What foundations and beliefs does this concept of a 'Soul-less being" upset? No Soul? No aeroship to carry you home? What can I be thinking to say such a thing? In the questioning mind, intelligence is born and bridges are built to the truth that will lead you home. Try to understand and envision what I mean when I speak of this "home." I have told you of a bridge to the Soul brain then introduced the possibility that there really is no Soul after all, no aeroship to carry you home. It is important for you to take the time now to identify and acknowledge what your beliefs are in this lifetime. Ask yourself what has kept you in this little box you call "reality." Look for answers. I will wait.

Do you believe you are this body? What if you are and that is all you are? Your current belief system allows you the tangibles of your five senses. What if that is all there is in your reality? You speak of love and hate, and you recognize that emotions reign supreme in the experiences of the human body. You pray. You have always been taught that there is a better place. You have only to be good and do good, and when you pass from this body you will be given your mansion of many rooms—your Valhalla; your resting place where all is possible. You will have peace. This is your heaven. Sound familiar?

Do you recall when first I spoke of Original Thought and that we were all sparks from that Original Thought? Do you remember? Tell me, does Original Thought have a Soul? Think about it. I can see the wheels turning, the beliefs from many lifetimes and experiences coming to the forefront. It is a known fact that when a human passes unto death, the body is lighter by so many ounces. That is the Soul leaving the body, is it not? I hear you cry, *I am not Soul-less! It cannot be.* This is quite a shake-up of your belief system. Let's go back to Original Thought and all the sparks that emanated from the Source, and let me ask you another question. Do you believe the sparks from Original Thought are limited, or do you believe that they continue to spark and ignite and create? It is yet another concept to consider. If you have accepted the concept of perpetual beginnings without end, then the mere fact that Original Thought exists would necessitate the continuing of the initial sparks and creation, would it not? But perhaps this is a concept to explore for another day.

Now, back to the Soul-less human entity. Hard to envision, isn't it? This is where I may lose some of you, for there are those who can only step out of their box of limits for a few safe realizations at a time. It is alright, and they are not to be judged by anyone. But this is truth I speak. The human, as a spark from Original Thought, is complete and whole from the beginning of inception. You are perfection, though this concept of perfection can bring to mind those occasions when the human appears to be anything but perfect. Wars perpetrated by man, genocide against one another in any form, pain, rapes, murders, to name but a few, are most painfully apparent in your world and have been almost from the beginning of recorded history. It may seem easier to crawl back into that box and cover yourself with the old belief systems than to take a chance and look too closely at new ideas. And yet I am pushing you to do just that—to look more closely.

You have come this far and journeyed with me outside the box and into all possibility. Now stay with me a bit longer, if you will. Do not allow limited beliefs to keep you bound. When I bring these realizations, these points to ponder into your consciousness, it is for a purpose. What might that purpose be? Today it is to ponder a Soul-less human. No aeroship to sail home on. No separate Self. I know it is difficult, but it is fully within your ability, if you so choose.

What will it mean to mankind if it is allowed to understand the concept of a Soul-less human? Will all belief systems crumble? Will foundations melt away? Will you find yourself naked in your beliefs and in fear of what may come next? Was the Soul and your ultimate redemption something you had counted on? Something to think about, isn't it? I have asked many questions and you have begun to contemplate this new concept from the perspective of the limited human self. In this process, you have begun to build a bridge from limited thought to unlimited thought. I have presented a very lofty teaching at this time. At this moment in your evolutionary process, you are ready to begin building these bridges. Hopefully, you will not run back into that box of limited mindset to hide. Stay with me for a while yet; we have made a very good start.

If you have no Soul and the beliefs that have been recorded throughout history to help solidify your journey were limited, what's wrong with that? If there is truly no aeroship to carry you home save your own mind, your own realizations and your own illumination, what then? I would say that instead of the belief of the Soul as a separate aeroship you may consider that you are privy to a greater truth right now. As Original Thought's creation, you are whole, you are perfect and you are taking everything

with you when you go. When you go? What does that mean? The body
appears to die and to be buried, does it not? Then what is it that leaves?
What goes on to become eternal? Please try to wrap your mind around
this concept. You have seen a snake shed its skin, have you not? Think
about it. What happens to the old skin? Doesn't the snake continue to live
with yet a new skin? This is a simplistic illustration of a very complicated
concept. You shed your human body because it is expected. It is a shared
belief of humans, so this scenario is played out. I am telling you now that
you remain a whole being when you leave or shed this body. There is no
separation. You are still Original Thought, you are still perfect and you
may choose to go on to take yet another form or to exist in the ethers as
light, sound and energy vibration. There is no separate Soul—only the
one perfect you from the beginning. No separate aeroship just the Self in
all its perfection.

This teaching was given to enable you to contemplate another avenue
of thought. It does not negate the concept of a Supreme Being, nor the
one called Jesus, nor any of the Saints or deities you worship, in whatever
religion you feel you need in order to survive. It is only a possibility that
I ask you to consider for now. Question everything that you have been
taught up to now and remain open for the new revelations to come. We are
building bridges, you and I; simply building bridges to new contemplations
of truth.

What I would like you to do with this information—this way out of "the
box"— is to simply be with it for awhile. For now, do not try to figure
it out or analyze it so you can prove me wrong. We are not in a contest.
Allow me the opportunity to present you with a way out of your limited
existence. Come forth into the act of being and believe in the Self. This
opportunity is being revealed to you in layers. You don't have to embrace
all that is given as truth. That is why so many questions are presented for
you to contemplate. You must always question what you are given. When
you can trust and accept each revelation as presented, as my scribe has done,
then you continue to move forward. She must accept, for now, without
question, in order to put it into words on the page. It doesn't mean she is
led like a sheep to slaughter; she is more like a partner. During our time
together, we are connected in a way that allows her to see the truth as it
is revealed. She sees between the lines that are presented on the page and

acknowledges what she has known from the beginning, as can you. We are not separate beings but whole entities that shed our skins, our bodies, from time-to-time. That is all. This is not intended to be blasphemous but simply truth to set you free. Do not be sheep that follow blindly. Question everything, for that is how you learn.

I have shaken the tree of your limited knowledge and asked you to consider yourself as whole from inception. We have been moving in the direction of this concept from the time we first began this journey together. Some of you will not choose to continue any further, but some of you will want to know what is next. And to those, all things are possible.

# CHAPTER SEVENTEEN

# THE EMERGING BUTTERFLY

At this specific time in the twenty-first century, human beings have the opportunity to come out of the chrysalis stage of metamorphosis and transform their lives forever. It is time to embrace the realm of truth and all possibility. It is also time to move beyond religious beliefs that have helped to shape the world in many subtle and not-so-subtle ways. Historically, religion has provided the rules and beliefs that justified many of their actions. Organized religions were often motivated more by the need to control the masses and enhance monetary gains than by the actual saving of your immortal Soul. You could say that religion had the world's first political agenda.

That you were birthed from something greater has been your faithful conviction from the inception of Original Thought. You have known from the time of your creation that you are unique and whole unto yourself. Your eternal light is pure and seeks only to seed the universal order through the love of the Self. You were birthed from that love and have dwelled in the cradle of wholeness from your beginning. You honor all things, especially the One who first placed you into the vastness of the void. Now you find yourself on a planet that has often used religion to promote weapons of hate or as a justification for war and punishment. I look upon those who gather to worship within these religious establishments and see these sparks of Original Thought merge into a single thought or belief determined by their leaders as truth. And I see the Self slowly and methodically becoming stifled.

There is an inferred sanctity of belief and goodness in every religious organization and a shared premise of one Supreme Being handing down laws to live by. These religions bring people together to teach their interpreted truths and expect them to honor the human who brings this wisdom. I watch you worship without question and see your spark dim with each moment that your uniqueness is controlled. I am challenging a belief system that has become deeply ingrained into the psyche of every spark that was ever birthed from Original Thought. And at the same time, I am attempting to instill the memory of how it was always intended to be.

While religious institutions have accomplished many good works, they still exert a form of mind-control over the true believers. Intentionally or not, they inhibit your spark, your unique Self, and the possibility you will ever remember at all. The original purpose of religion was to maintain control over those who would remember the Self. Sadly, it proved all too easy to usurp your uniqueness. Thinking for oneself became counter-productive to the group, so individual thought was stifled. Fostered instead was a belief system that negated everything that was not part of the order prescribed by a group leader.

I have brought this to your attention now because you have many competing belief systems pulling at you at once and must decide where to place your focus. Why should you believe what I speak? Am I not just one more voice attempting to enlighten you? Is this not what religion has always promised to do? Why should you listen to me and the seemingly blasphemous utterances that I have brought forth on these pages? Who can you trust, and how can you begin to live the realization that you are whole and unique once more? These are good questions. I do not want you to worship me or any of the guides and teachers that are known to you. My purpose is to bring you back to your original Self. My purpose is to lay before you the places you have been, what you have created, your belief systems, your joys and your sorrows. I have brought these before you to contemplate, and now I want you to forget everything. I want you to forget your past and your future and now simply be that spark of Original Thought with all potential intact. Can you? I would ask you, as I did in the beginning, to Come forth into the act of being and believe in the Self. *The Self is the spark of your original form.* The Self is complete and unique. It is not in the process of becoming; it simply *Is.* I would ask you to forever *come forth*. My purpose will always be to bring you back to the Source of all truth and possibility when you forget to remember.

Do not build a religion around what you are being taught. Do not worship or bow down to the one who brings you this wisdom. Look kindly upon the one who helps you to remember, and then be on your way. Gather together with those of like mind and purpose. It is there you will find support when you forget to remember. Allow each their individual journey as you continue to move in a forward motion. You are presently experiencing only a very small portion of your birthed potential, but you have opened the floodgates and allowed these truths to pour in. You will not drown but instead float above the fray and be carried on the wings of truth. Your old foundations, built on sand and half-truths, are crumbling. Your beliefs and your icons are being challenged. You have been told to come forth, and so you have. I have not spoken falsely; I speak only the truth that you have known from the beginning. Why do I continue to bring you back to the very beginning? Because you are willing to go, and that is an auspicious opportunity indeed.

Take these teachings and contemplate them for a bit. I may not tell you much you don't already know, but I will attempt to add another layer of truth to what you have been given up to now, and, in the process, explore many layers to see the deeper meaning. It is the way it must be, so we can get to the core of the Self once more. Religious establishments have not always brought peace, love and goodness to the world. Whenever I strike down a faulty belief, it is to reveal the Divine spark hiding beneath the cloak of forgetfulness. You are the Self, and I am here to reveal it all. And you are here to remember.

You have been learning to shed those concepts and beliefs that keep you frozen in time, repeating over and over identical scenarios and puppet lifetimes. It is time to step out of that mold and embrace the Self in all its abundant glory. How will the truth be revealed? It is a process like anything of great worth. It sustains itself and grows in meaning, as you move forward revealing the half-truths and falsehoods that have kept you bound. You cannot learn to fly without first being shoved out of the nest, so to speak. If you observe the animal kingdom, you will gain an understanding of what I mean. The animal baby is nurtured with life-sustaining liquid and nutrients and then released from this state of dependence into the world of Self journey. The human process is similar. Birthed from the All Knowing into the universal order, you are nurtured and fed and sent out to become complete in your own right, while in accord with Original Thought's intent.

We have spoken often of what it means to *Come forth into the act of being and believe in the Self*. Everything that has been presented thus far has been based on this mantra of the highest order. Practice the act of being and believe in the Self, and come home.

CHAPTER EIGHTEEN

# THE SPIRIT SELF

The Spirit and Soul are separate, yet have always been spoken of within the same context and understanding. This is not an accurate assumption, and I will tell you why. There is no part of you that is separate from the Self. You are One, in the embrace of the Spirit that surrounds you and encompasses every aspect of your Being; you are One with Original Thought. Spirit is the binding that surrounds your spark, your vibrational life energy. Spirit is not separate from the human body but part of every cloak you wear and every lifetime you live. Every fiber of your being is filled and embraced by the Spirit of the Self. It is not the aeroship that will carry you home but simply *Is*. It requires no aeroship save the Self, all tied up in the ribbon called "Spirit." Spirit ties a bow quite nicely around this planet as it weaves itself into the fabric of your lives. But it is different from your understanding of the Soul.

The Soul is believed to command and transcend the Self in death, but it is your Spirit that surrounds and is infused within the Self. You never shed the skin of the Spirit. It is your spark, your guidepost and your realization that the Self lives on without end. It is to your Spirit I speak, for it is the purest form of the Self. Spirit is your individual tone of universal vibration. Unique. Complete. Whole. You are truly the Spirit Self and never separate from Original Thought's intention. When you shed the skin of human existence, the Spirit remains constant and is with you whenever and wherever you may choose to be. Your continued growth and expansion is at your command. The Spirit stays with you and is truly who you are. You spark with energy, sound and light. You are Original Thought personified, wrapped in the package called "Spirit," constantly moving out into the Universal Order to embrace all possibility.

The Self knows and remembers everything. The Self comes with Spirit as a partner for each cloak that is worn, each lifetime lived. The Self retains all memory, every lifetime lived and housed in your unconscious mind. The unconscious mind—the Self of Original Thought—when paired with conscious mind, caused a division of truth. When I speak of the need to combine the two minds into one True Mind, it is to help eliminate any concept of separation. There has only ever been Original Thought, the one that gave birth to us all. You are not the limited, often confused, thought processes of your conscious mind. It truly doesn't matter how you came to this point in time; what matters is how you will continue to evolve.

To begin to live the True Mind experience, first think of it as already part of your reality. The conscious mind thinks the True Mind must be something tangible to be considered authentic. The unconscious mind accepts the truth, while the conscious mind continues to live in relative ignorance, finding no justification to explore further. We have come to set the wind to your sails and to see you captain your ship along the path of truth. When you are asked to come forth into the act of being and believe in the Self you are doing just that.

Recognize the truth as stated—you are Spirit, Original Thought and one True Mind. The Spirit is made up of the cells of the universal order and, as such, holds all truth and knowledge. When you have the opportunity to play in the realm of the human and to experience life on this planet, you retain all universal memory sheathed within Spirit. When told to come forth into the act of being, you are asked to believe in the Self. For some of you, living the truth of one True Mind and integrating it into your life experience is a difficult task to accomplish. It is why we are here now on your planet in such numbers.

Living in this human body on planet earth, you made an agreement to live within a set of limits. Your beliefs order your world and give you a sense of stability and focus in which to function and interact within your environment. You believe that up is up and down is down, that there is good and there is evil and that opposites and separation exist. You live by the rules and have even agreed to exceptions to those rules. And everything in your world is right-side- up as you live each day and learn from your experiences. This is your world, the planet earth, the life that you have chosen, and you are deeply ingrained in this life. And yet, here you are, searching and moving beyond this well-ordered space, willing to step out of one reality and into another, if only for a moment, and willing to expand and explore the concept of the Self.

If one is to be enlightened, one must bring together the many abilities and insights that the Self possesses. You are the Self. You are birthed from Original Thought and carry all knowledge within the cells of your Being. What does it mean to "be enlightened"? It means that you have the willingness, the ability and preparedness to reach this place of Oneness once more. Being *willing* is a very important state of awareness that most who say they wish to be enlightened have not yet achieved. To be willing is to have the discipline of mind, body and Spirit, as well as the desire to go beyond perceived limitations. What will be achieved as a result is that moment of convergence called "enlightenment." This is the place where you exist beyond limits, envision with eyes that do not see and listen with ears that do not hear—save for the All that birthed you.

When your discipline joins with the desire and willingness to learn, all things are possible. It really is up to you. The decision for such a completeness to occur is not always made consciously, so I have taught you about the True Mind, where both minds are joined into one. The ability to understand the events that occur to facilitate enlightenment is housed within the True Mind, integrated into Spirit body and finally embraced by the All as One. Is this state of enlightenment the sole purpose of your journey? Not at all. But it is important to become acquainted with each level of knowledge as presented for your further understanding and then move on. There is still much to learn beyond this place of enlightenment. For now, *act as if* you are without limit and envision your expansion into the realm of all possibility.

We will not dwell on this idea of enlightenment but will use this awareness as a steppingstone to further expand the Self. Never limit yourself to one idea or one belief system. Accept what you can now and keep moving forward, because there is always more to learn. There are many who do not journey much beyond a single awareness. I seek those who wish to continue searching and expanding all possibility and truth. To be enlightened is not our main goal. The process of awakening is as important as reaching this so-called "state of enlightenment." Do not get lost in the idea of enlightenment. Do not get lost in the drive to become One with the All, because you already are this One. Enlightenment can occur for you in every truth you uncover. It is that "Ah-ha!" moment shared between your conscious and unconscious, as the joining of the two become the True Mind experience. You are not to be concerned with things that do not matter or any preconceived notions of what enlightenment should be. I will not provide a resting platform of beliefs to sit upon, where you may linger with your misconceptions, but will help to dispel preconceived notions deeply engrained in the conscious mind. Enlightenment is only one stage of consciousness where the Self can be revealed.

You are enlightened when a previously unknown truth is integrated into your consciousness. At one time, my scribe experienced a period of clumsiness that she called being "out of balance." It was an apt description to be sure, which occurred as a result of a shift in her conscious awareness. She was literally out of balance, dizzy and unable to navigate in her environment, and it took her several days to realign. When these subtle moments of enlightenment occur and this shift in awareness is integrated, new avenues of learning open up. This shift enabled further information to come through on this subject, as she was able to understand and integrate her own experience firsthand. For now, simply view enlightenment as steps along the way to greater evolution.

This world of yours is going through countless changes. The stage has been set for many great Masters to emerge from among you to teach and show the way through the multiple levels of enlightenment. These Masters will teach what for some may seem blasphemous. Still, there will be those who accept these messages, embrace these new ideas and continue to grow. It is to those we speak. Take heart in the knowledge that you are truly moving forward and forever embracing a journey of new beginnings. As you walk your path, I ask you to bring laughter and light to your surroundings and illume the space in which you dwell. Never hide. Accept who you are in truth, and come forth with a loving, sharing attitude. Observe what happens when you no longer hold back the light that you are but share it openly. This can also be done silently, starting with a simple prayer:

*Let my light shine brightly on this day and embrace all of mankind in truth, enlightenment and love.*

From just such a place of intention, all things are possible. When one is privy to knowledge such as this, there is a certain obligation to follow wherever the path may lead you.

You have come to a place in time when many things that you previously believed to be true are now something else entirely. You may continue trying to fit a square peg into a round hole but find that it just doesn't work any longer. You have always lived a life of your own design, but I have come now, as have many, to shake you up. We will continue to tell you simple truths that are intended to dispel the myths of your existence in this dimension. When the world seems too much to handle, you need to sit in silence and be at peace. If you have determined this journey worth your while, important to your path and your place in the universal order, then come forth and meet the destiny that was promised long ago. When you feel the need to contemplate and integrate a new concept, take the time to do so. You must always take care of the one who is on this journey.

For each of you, there are guides and teachers available at all times—from birth to death and beyond even that. Some call these beings "guardian angels," though that hardly describes them accurately. These Spirit Beings come to you when called upon in earnest by the Self. They do so from the absolute love of humanity as a whole and a specific connection to the one who calls them forth. You are never completely alone. This is how, in your infinite wisdom, you planned it to be. You created guides to help when you forget to remember your connection to Original Thought. Once in awhile, you allow these guides to speak to you through your inner knowing, and it is at times like these, when you surrender to this knowing, that the greatest lessons can be learned. I have come to this scribe after another guide, whom she called Ezekiel, had been with her for a very long time. I entered into this "guide business" to bring certain information forth at this time—to assist in the growth of the Self in awareness—and had been with her for some time before I was acknowledged. She has made herself available now to scribe in earnest what it is we have to convey.

*Come forth into the act of being and believe in the Self* is mankind's daily lesson. Assimilate and activate that realization and live it as truth. I come to my scribe as words on a page. There is no visible form for her to gaze upon; there is only my scribe embracing the Self, quietly seated before her computer. I speak words that cannot be physically heard but must be internalized and translated within the conscious mind and recorded as words on the page. This method of listening occurs in a different dimension than the one ordinarily experienced. Are these words the truth? Are they the musings of a saint, a madman, a god? She no longer questions. She has learned to believe and trust in the Self, and simply listen and type the wisdom as given.

When you attempt to listen with "ears that do not hear," it simply means that you are not hearing with your physical ears but are receiving the *energy* of the word, as well as the word itself. From within that space of a higher dimensional existence, you see many different layers of meaning at the same time. Moving in and out of dimensional realities, you are able to experience the abilities and freedoms present at each level. Some of you have been moving rapidly between dimensional realities on a daily basis in the waking state you call "earthbound human" and in what you call "the dream." We acknowledge those who have chosen this adventure, and work with them from within their understanding. When you are journeying within a higher existence, you have given permission to the Self to come forth into the act of being and live this truth in every moment.

It is time to move forward and leave behind what no longer fits within your conscious reality. Continue to be the observer and pay attention to everything. Maintain your forward momentum and embrace new visions of truth. Remember, you are not your emotions but simply the Self awakening. When you are about the Self and totally absorbed in the journey, you become more expansive and able to live your life with more joy and purpose. What has concerned you before begins to fall away. Be the observer of the people closest to you. Send them love and surround them with the continuing Light of peace and truth, but do not become attached to their outcome.

The journey of being about the Self doesn't mean that you must live in a cave in the mountains or in an ashram, or anywhere but *where you already are*. You are shedding the cloak of blind conviction and becoming a Self-actualized being. In the process, you will become more loving and accepting of everything in your life from a new perspective of truth. You will allow it all but demand much in return. Sounds like a dichotomy, doesn't it? It isn't. In your allowance, you have chosen to keep your own counsel and to separate from outside emotion. What you will demand of yourself will be complete autonomy. You will be wholly immersed in the concept of the Self, in the act of being, until such time as you can embrace it in truth. In reality, you are not on a single journey but on many journeys simultaneously. But for now, this is your primary focus.

Practice becoming detached. Begin to shed the feeling that this sense of detachment evokes in you. When you detach from the drama around you, it will set you free. Yes, I know your mind is saying, "But I am not attached, and I do remove myself from other people's emotions." I would only ask you to be the observer and steadfastly honest in your observations. If you can truly observe what surrounds you at any given moment, view it with love and send forth the Light of peace, then good for you! It would be my guess that perhaps you have a little more to learn. However, it is your observation of the truth we are after, not mine, and I will trust your judgment. You have your ongoing assignment for now. Do not judge the process or what you bring to it. In the midst of observation, you will begin to come forth into the act of being. Then you will know what it is you must learn from each and every experience before you. It is you who provides the experience, not I. I am only the observer who helps you gain insight from what you observe. You are, as ever, the captain of your ship.

CHAPTER NINETEEN

# REVELATION

What if the Book of Revelation is not about the destruction of mankind but, instead, is an attempt to reveal a much different truth? What if the "rapture" simply depicts the existence of multiple realities and its purpose is to lift you up into expanded consciousness? For those of you who are willing to experience these dimensional layers, it is indeed a revelation. While death, destruction, wars and earth's upheaval are all part of the Book of Revelation, your human mind is also being asked to see the illusion of this single-dimensional existence in which you live. What if this is possibly one of the most revealing books of sacred truth in the Bible?

The Book of Revelation has stirred the Christian consciousness as no other has save that of the resurrection of Christ. Some believe it describes the heavenly assent of all who believe in a certain doctrine and, at the same time, punishes those who do not share this narrow view. The described war that rages is purportedly between good and evil and the fight for the human soul. What if the Book of Revelation, instead, is meant to reveal that God lives within each and every one of us as a spark of Original Thought? What if the upheaval predicted is, in truth, the end of separation of the two minds and the rapture an illustration of the True Mind experience? And what if this created a joy of such intensity and magnitude that you were uplifted from limited human experience into one of All Knowing? You would truly never be the same. The Book of Revelation has been universally interpreted to go with certain beliefs and religious doctrines. I have just told you my truth and given you yet another interpretation to consider.

Be the observer of any controversy or confusion this interpretation might bring and then, as always, keep moving forward.

There are those from the Spirit world who come in many guises to impart great wisdom for any who will listen. The truth spoken is what you are in reality—not a limited being in human form, but *unlimited* potential. Though this may seem a rather simplified statement, herein lies the truth. It is from Spiritual guidance such as this that you will find the wisdom needed to conduct your life in enlightened truth and experience. Enlightenment is simply living truth as you know it to be.

What if the competition that rages inside you between the conscious and unconscious minds is the ultimate betrayal—an elaborate illusion or ruse, if you will—that is meant to keep you bound in this reality? What if, in actuality, there is no conscious or unconscious mind? If this is true, then it would follow that True Mind would not be a combination of these two minds but something else entirely—perhaps something far grander than you can yet imagine. Just by allowing this possibility, you make way for further enlightened truths to be introduced in the future.

I have planted yet another seed for growth. Now, having deprived you of the accepted belief in the conscious and unconscious mind, you might ask where you are expected to seed this new concept. This is a very good question, so for now simply place this seed within the parameters of all possibility and truth, and leave the illusion of separate minds behind. Let the temporal lobe vision pull you through the threshold of the seeking mind to the True Mind revealed. What if the Book of Revelation was written to reveal the truth of the True Mind's existence and was meant only for those who would go beyond its obvious interpretation? If what I speak is true, how does it change the way in which you live your life now? At this moment, it may not change it very much at all. But I will continue to plant such seeds for your contemplation, and you will let them germinate as long as you must, for time is an illusion.

You have allowed another door to open. When a truth such as this is discovered, it becomes your personal revelation and you are forever changed. This is your rapture. The process will take as long as it takes until the bloom of truth is fully upon you. Some Christian faiths believe that during the rapture your clothes will fall from your body as you are taken up into heaven. Perhaps this "falling away of limitation" will reveal all that you are—all that is your heaven, your truth and your peace.

I have told you that you are a spark from Original Thought and, as such, have the ability to lay claim to the All. You have been asked to look at the Soul as a non-entity and the conscious and unconscious mind as human creations for life on this planet. Piece by piece, the foundation upon which you have based your understanding of truth will be removed until all that remains is the concept of the Self. What is stripped away is superfluous to the uncovering of enlightened truth. The Self is not only the vehicle that will bring you home, it is your home, your beginning without end and all the experiences in between. You are always beginning, for, in truth, there is no ending time—only a time for truth to be revealed. When the journey of the Self is lived as a single purpose, you are able to free yourself from all falsehood and limitation. The journey of the Self illuminates every thought and belief that you have ever explored. Nothing can hide from this illumed light in the darkness of deception because there are no shadows there to conceal the truth.

The True Mind is not a combination of the conscious and unconscious but, in fact, is absolute. It is a part of the Self and, as such, can have no opposite. Opposites were created when you became entangled here on your planet. From the time of your birth into Being, there have only been these prevailing truths: You are love and you are loved; you are whole; you are complete; you are the spark from the Divine. There is nothing else, save what has been created by you to journey. Creating such a dichotomy as two minds and the opposites of love, light and truth was an experiment. You learned from this, but you also forgot much in the process. And so it has been necessary to bring you back to the very beginning and strip away your mistaken beliefs, one by one, so we may begin again, for I have told you we are always beginning.

You may be wondering if mankind has done this before, and I would tell you absolutely. Many, many, many times. And on each occasion a different result has been the outcome. You have never failed in any of your attempts, only gained greater wisdom. And now, once again, we must wipe the slate clean of what you have believed to be true. You have heard that history often repeats itself, but do you know why? History repeats itself until it is refined to such an extent that all that can be gleaned from any experience is fully integrated, with no further need to repeat the lesson, and freeing you to move forward. Your planet has been at this place in its evolutionary journey many times and on some occasions been destroyed. But when new truth is brought forth and expanded, the subtle changes made to future outcomes have allowed your planet's journey to continue. This time around, new possibilities and truths are being realized every day. A Hitler didn't win the war, and earthquakes and volcanic eruptions that would have torn the earth asunder were avoided. Though some natural disasters continue to happen—as well as wars, death and destruction—it has not produced the same outcome as before. You have been set free from what has come before and been able to create from a new realization of the Self that is coming to fruition. This time around, you have begun to awaken more fully and allowed enlightened truth to come forth. Jesus didn't always have to die on the cross you know, but this time it gained the attention of those who built a following around Him, which changed the makeup and future of many events. There are those from the Spirit realm who are dedicated to earth's evolution and have come to live again as human, specifically for the opportunity to influence and experience the altering of current reality. Earth's evolution has not gone unnoticed throughout the universal order, and many visitations from other planets and universes have occurred. Everyone is about minding everyone else's business, for that is how learning takes place and is solidified in the consciousness of man.

Great experimentations are afoot. Some might say that events that bring pain, death, loss and hatred are not experiments that need to be repeated. Such events are the product of beings that have come without conscious awareness of the Self and go about playing irresponsibly with the lives of others as well as their own. I speak the truth when I say that you're not separate minds or a separate Soul but, rather, Spirit beings—whole, complete, Original Thought and the spark of the Divine. You experience life for the elevation and growth of your Spirit-Self and will create what you need in order to continue your forward momentum. However, when you are manifesting creations from the collective consciousness that are supported by more than a single mind intention, it may be more difficult to move beyond them. When this happens, the creation manifests and grows on its own. Then a Hitler is born and allowed to bring chaos on a grand scale until all who have created this experiment agree to eliminate the destructive force of group intent. As you play in the field of God, many such individual and global events are experienced.

Go and be with this truth for a while yet. Do not trouble your mind. I have given you much to contemplate, which is why I have brought it forth to be seeded at this time. Many of you already accept that you create your own reality. What I have introduced today also concerns your collective, group projections. This will assist you to look at your life and see the complicated interactions that can result from living these group manifestations. There are many such experiences woven into your reality at this time. Though you may have had little experience integrating and identifying enlightened truth, you have made a very good beginning. The unraveling of group-mind deception will help to set you on a new path of enlightened truth and purpose.

CHAPTER TWENTY

# THE SPIRIT-SOUL

The term "death" often carries with it an ominous meaning for something that is truly transformational. This word is used to describe what happens to the human body when the Spirit-Soul leaves and ascends into heaven. Death, in one form or another, is found in every civilization, galaxy and planetary body in the universal order. For our purpose, we will use the term "Spirit-Soul" to reference what passes from the body at the time of death. When death occurs, the Spirit-Soul is lifted up and out of the human body and given the opportunity to view life from a different perspective. It is a transformational experience without limit or form, which allows one to seek the true origin of their birth. If the Spirit-Soul is willing, it is quickly taken to its beginning spark of realization and moved forward through all it has experienced. It can happen in an instant when one is not bound by conventional time and space.

Sometimes Spirit-Souls choose to remain close to what has been familiar before they fully transition. Their ghostly forms see but cannot be seen by most. They may be afraid to let go of human reality, not trusting what is in store for them beyond their physical lifetime of order and convention, friends, family and familiar places. For them, death is not a time of joy and reunion with Source. When facing death, most will struggle to live, afraid to let go of all that is familiar. But they are the spark from Original Thought and, as such, have lived and existed since the beginning of creation.

Picture, if you will, one who has recently passed from the body. He has been taken back to Original Thought or Source, experienced all known truth and then found himself back among the living... but with one difference: the living cannot see him. While he may visit his own funeral and observe the grief of those he loves, he is strangely unaffected emotionally because he is viewing it all from another perspective. Still, he may choose to linger, and walk the familiar pathways of his old life. It is much like the reluctance one has to getting rid of a favorite old pair of shoes or sweater. The usefulness of these items has long since passed, but the comfort of having them still lingers. Some of these ghostly apparitions are simply lingering Spirit-Souls that are unwilling to let go of what is familiar in order to embrace the light of a far greater truth. Until they can turn toward this light and those who wait to lead them home, they won't move past the attachments of this lifetime. Once they accept what is before them, their true life begins. It is simple really—just view each lifetime experience as if you are putting on a cloak and wearing it for only a short while, then taking it off when you pass from that life and continuing on as before. There is always a "before" to each lifetime lived, and always the Original Thought that awaits your return. This cloak is your experiential human life and can be worn many different times and then shed at will through your divine intention. Death is simply removing that cloak while your true life continues.

Come forth into the act of being and believe in the Self. It is the only truth for you now, until you are ready to move beyond even that limit. Do not be fearful of the coming dawn of enlightenment. Do not resist information that will transform the reality of now into the truth of tomorrow. Do not be afraid. You may think you are without fear, but each moment you live in human form, fear is ever-present in the mind. The fear I speak of is not what might occur from an accident, loss, violence or any natural disaster; these fears are only transitory. The fear I speak of is the deep-seated fear of never again connecting completely to the truth of who you are, your Original Self. This truth resonates with force and energy within every cell of your body, and does so from the time one incarnates from Spirit into form. When I say to you, "Do not be afraid," it is to remind you that this fear exists. Only by acknowledging this fear are you able to bring it into the conscious mind and the truth of your existence.

Let us deal now with the fear that some may have of connecting to the truth. I have observed the current rhetoric on your planet concerning the subject of enlightenment from the spiritual and religious beliefs of today. It appears that many of these beliefs are built on fear. There is fear of death, fear of hell, fear of not being good enough, fear of the devil, ad infinitum. More often than not, these fears are planted in an attempt to cultivate a need for dependency, and you become dependent on certain organizations to run your life and give you the parameters within which to judge what is right and what is wrong. You often seek someone to lay out your life plan, yet never consider that perhaps your life plan has already been made from a much higher perspective. Is the one who planned your life the Supreme Being? Of course. And that Supreme Being is *you*, yet you have put yourself in the position of seeker and become subordinate to what you believe to be a more powerful wisdom. You seek the one who will tell you what to believe, who to trust and what to fear. It is quite a difficult path you walk, and this struggle is totally unnecessary.

I do not expect you to isolate yourself or never seek counsel or become part of a group that has similar goals and beliefs, but I would always caution you to find your Divine truth within any teaching you choose to follow. How you accomplish this is up to you. Come forth with a readiness and a willingness to learn, but never do so from fear. There are many wonderful and loving teachers available to you at this time as there have been throughout your history. You may find their teachings in many enlightened books or group lectures, even from the pulpits of your organized religions. Some of your religious leaders are very enlightened and are part of a new guard coming forth into the upper echelons of your spiritual and religious hierarchy. These priests, rabbis, preachers and mullahs are less dogmatic and are collectively open to enlightened spiritual truth. These beings have infiltrated, if you will, the religious orders that are the most influential at this time, and are making quiet inroads toward a system of more universal truths that will prevail in the coming years. These inroads into the religious philosophy and doctrines of the churches, mosques and synagogues of your day will test the waters of a new dawn. Peace will be possible on this planet—true peace—when those who speak from their pulpits acknowledge enlightened spiritual truth and share it with those who seek their counsel. It will be quite a revolution. Look for evidence of these first steps in your newspapers and on your media. These will be very small stories at first, and they will stir up little controversy. As we speak, the power struggle within these establishments is ongoing and the outcome not certain. But I know the outcome. I have seen it, and I know that truth is upon you.

This is an exciting time for your planet—a good time to be alive and present here. It is a time when many humans are coming alive and welcoming spiritual truth back into there lives. Increasing numbers are seeking to transcend this fear-based society, to remember and seed the truth from these experiences into everyday life. In this way, fear will be overcome, and it will be a release of great magnitude. At first, it may be hard to change this habit of fear, but admitting it is currently part of your global society is the first step in allowing you to move beyond it.

Life is transitory. You must always seek to remember from whence you came, for in the midst of living life, much can be forgotten. What can be forgotten is the wonder and purpose of the Spirit-Soul specifically created to guide you through life's transitions. What is transitory is the human form that sheaths the Spirit-Soul. The Spirit-Soul gathers up the sparking energy vibration that is you and forms it into a tiny human birthed from the womb of a mother. It is truly a wonder that the human body can contain such beauty! When one is willing to search out his beginning— the starting point of his existence—true vision and purpose can emerge.

Fear is ever-present in the mind of the human. There may be the fear of sickness, death or lack of money, security or shelter. Some may fear for their safety. So many fears and so few, in actuality, created outside the Self. You may ask why the Self would create such distractions and place the focus on fear instead of discovery? I would answer that it has to do with memory loss—but not in the sense of forgetting someone's birthday or an appointment. This greater loss of memory is forgetting to remember what the Spirit-Soul is about and the knowledge of what Original Thought has created. You cannot truly lose what is part of you. And, in reality, the Spirit-Soul is the only part of you that is of any true substance. It may be confusing to think of the Spirit-Soul as "substance," but it is the only thing about you that is truly real. So what do you suppose all this fear is about?

In the beginning—the true beginning, when Original Thought came alive and you were born into the vastness of the newly forming universe— you were without fear. You played in the field of sound and light and vibrational energy, and were a part of everything. But now you are here in human form, fear keeps you stuck, afraid to explore and to remember this beginning time. Fear keeps you living within your box of limits, yet every time you allow a new truth to be acknowledged, it penetrates and dissipates the thick layer of fear that surrounds you. Then the light shines through and your true Self is revealed.

You haven't the power to change the journey or direction of anyone in your life, for everyone walks a path of Self-awareness in their own individual way. You may question why certain events happen that prevent a peaceful and happy life. I would tell you that it is fear that keeps you bound to perpetuating these scenarios. These fears lie buried deep within a mind that has ceased to be an instrument of remembering the connection to the All. Instead, your mind has become a storehouse of experiences that you revisit every time you attempt to progress in a forward motion. If this sounds daunting, remember that illumed knowledge is the key that allows you to move beyond fear. The mind can be viewed as a jailer that keeps you locked up in your fear. You are released when light penetrates the walls of your cell and the door to truth is opened. It is quite telling that a cell of the human body and the cell of a prison should have similar names. In each case, the cell in question contains the complete Self.

I speak to you about fear at length and quite often because it is so much a part of your human life. Each time a barrier is created, fear is present; yin and yang, black and white. Opposites. Always you must deal with opposites until you discover that there is only one truth—Original Thought and all life contained in the single cell. There is no prison of the mind that can contain what you are. The mind can work as your jailer, or it can set you free. I encourage you to harness the mind and come out of that jail cell where you have lived far too long. We have begun to swing the door wide open. Now it is your job to pass through it willingly. Do not fear what you do not remember, for in the process of your discovery of Divine truth, your greatest adventure begins.

Journey with me and do not stop too long to gather the flowers along your path. We are in a forward march and will not be detained by things that are of little importance—even though these experiences are part of the pattern of your life. Only in this continued momentum will you discover your truth. You create experiences as you live your life, and you learn from them. There is always a new beginning and a new dawn of enlightened awareness to experience. When you become sidetracked, gathering flowers and creating diversions, fear has a chance to take control. Pay attention and stay focused on the exercise of forward momentum, and your fear will be eliminated through Divine contemplation.

CHAPTER TWENTY-ONE

# ALL POSSIBILITIES

As the events of your life become one with your Spirit-Soul, they are absorbed within the vibrational pulse and rhythm of the universal order. When challenges arise that disrupt this flow, certain irritations may occur. And just as the pearl is formed from irritation in the mantle of an oysters shell, something beautiful emerges. Throughout your life, you may encounter many irritations and frustrations of growth potential. How you deal with them will tell the tale of your existence. When you face these challenges using Divine truth and trust the decisions you make, you will experience your ultimate potential for growth. The pearl of your true life will begin to appear. It is important not to judge any of these events but embrace the wisdom of their creation and then journey what has been placed before you in truth.

Throughout the ages, I have had the opportunity to observe many religious and spiritual communities and their master teachers. Each of these institutions and teachers has brought to the populous their interpretation of the purpose and meaning of life. As a result, they have given you a framework for living which ultimately contributed to the building of your box of ideals, rules and regulations. You were cautioned to think with one collective consciousness and were often punished when you didn't conform. Nonetheless, some of you stepped out of that box, and we were happy to greet you when you did. When one is a seeker of truth, the truth is revealed. Mankind is experiencing an upheaval that will reshape the thinking and inevitable outcome of your planet's journey and the purpose of living wholly in truth. When you live this journey, the expanded view of truth that opens before you is vast indeed. You have only to sit and dream this dream of truth and it will become your reality.

At present, certain experiences on this planet are created wholly from youthful thinking. What is youthful thinking? These are the thoughts and creations made from the perspective of one who is on the cusp of maturity and full knowledge of truth. Mankind, you are truly just entering the beginning stages of puberty. Even though I have told you of the beginning of your creation as a planet and the billions of years of creative force that has taken place, your planet and its inhabitants are indeed youthful in many ways. I speak of this now because it is time to grow up. There are some teachers who have brought the wisdom of worlds beyond this one and of time that is not counted in seconds, minutes, hours or days. They have spoken of the act of creating. They have told you that where you find yourself now is the dream and the reality is what you have yet to remember or realize. I have been such a teacher myself. All this knowledge and discovery was for a purpose. Once gained, this journey needs to keep moving forward to reveal more serious contemplations of truth.

You are residing on this planet at this time for a specific purpose. One of your popular sayings is "Life happens." This is true. Life does happen, and how you deal with the day-to-day experiences determine the stage of your evolutionary progress. Evolutionary change is upon you. Forget all that you have been told, and wipe the slate clean. Take an honest look at where you are and who you are at this very moment. Tell me what you believe to be your truth, and I will tell you that at this very moment in time you are exactly who you were meant to be. Are you one who can heal life, or are you one who takes it? If you are a healer, must you always be one? If you are one who takes life, must you always do so? What is your life plan, and can it be changed? That is the ultimate question, is it not?

You have been told by learned teachers that you are the author of your life plan. If that is so, why would you ever plan to be sick, poor, lonely or in pain? Why would you choose a life that would limit your thinking or create prejudice of any kind? When Original Thought scattered the sparks of Its Being out into the void and the universal plan began, did you imagine your life would turn into a tally sheet of do's and don'ts with a record kept of all you had ever been, all your failures and all your successes?

It is a truth that many ascribe to. But what if I told you that that was never the intent and this belief system is a limit that keeps you perpetuating the lie of reincarnation? Reincarnation, or the concept of rebirth, was used as a control imposed upon mankind to perpetuate the further limit of rehashing and revisiting earth to right imaginary wrongs. Why would you come only to experience a life plan that would deny you the opportunity to expand beyond this limited imaginary and false hope? Why, indeed?

Tell me what you know for certain at this moment. Have I taken from you the hope for a better life next time around? Can you continue to accept living here, knowing you won't have to account for all your so-called failures when your body dies? Or can you simply slip from this earth upon death and rejoin the liquid vibrational pulse of Original Thought in a welcome homecoming? More than likely, you will experience whatever you believe the truth to be. *The concept of reincarnation to right imagined wrongs is a fallacy.* There is no one to take the accounting of your previous lifetimes except *you*, the Self, although guidance from kindred beings of light is always available, if you so desire. The sights and sounds and colors that await you upon your return to Original Thought cannot be adequately described or even imagined from your human perspective. While it remains difficult to leave this place of beautiful peace and once again enter into existence on this earthly planet, you often choose to do so. The experiences you have don't need to be complicated or generate an accounting, a record or a limit of any kind for you to journey. The truth is as it has always been: you are a spark from Original Thought and, as such, have complete freedom to journey. The universe is filled with opportunity. You are simply playing in the garden of all possibility.

When an actor takes on a character in a play and wears the costume of that identity and performs the play that was written, the space around him is affected by each action, each word, each thought and portrayal according to the script. Perhaps you can think of reincarnation in that way—simply acts in a play of your choosing. While you are the author of this play and the ultimate power of creative force, you also created a judging God within the parameters of your box of limits. But I see you as you have always been—without shadow, doubt or any misconceptions clouding your vision. Some of you stand before me, free from the cloak of false truth and ready to take on each new revelation. Though there may be many questions in your mind, you continue to move forward, trusting they will be answered. More often than not, they will be answered by your awakening Spirit. Removing the blinders from your eyes allows you to live your journey from a more in-depth level of understanding. As you begin to remove the veils of misconception and limit from your human mind, you have the opportunity to realize the truth of the Self and Original Thought, which is the beginning, the middle and the end that will never be.

There are humans on this planet who create and live lives that are successful and bring them contentment. There is never a desire to move much beyond what is familiar or comfortable, and they become resistant to anything outside their parameters of truth. Anything outside their truth can be seen as a threat to their way of life and belief system. Throughout your history, there have been individuals who have led nations and their people into some horrendous wars and genocidal atrocities. The fear is great in those who attempt to control others with force. They have a driving need to contain any stray thoughts which might prove contrary to their belief. What is also true, in the midst of such chaos, is the work of some enlightened Spirit-Souls who bravely speak the words and perform the actions that heal such fear and change the face of humanity forever.

Sometimes it may seem that the journey of the Self is the only place of peace found within the madness of the life that surrounds you. I have heard the phrase "a strong sense of self" used to describe individuals who believe strongly in who they are, in spite of any outside interference or turmoil they may encounter. When one has this innate sense of the Self, acts upon it, journeys in spite of restrictions and allows new experience without resistance, the true wonders of Original Thought are realized. Breaking out of self-imposed limit can be as difficult or as easy as one makes it. And if these limits are exactly where the Self wishes to reside, then that is what the Self will journey. Those who are content to journey the Self within limited desire live on in a continuing wheel of birth and rebirth. It is a cycle of similarity, emotional restriction and experiences that support the humans' beliefs. But there are those who choose to explore other realms and the far-reaching peaks and valleys of the Self, to create lives of all possibility rather than recreate similar experiences. Is one life better than the other? Of course not. This adventure is about the Self and the choices made are individual and not to be judged. The Self is unique. There is no right or wrong, only journey. This can be difficult to comprehend when one believes in the concept of opposites, but it is the truth nonetheless. It was always intended that you have all possibilities available to you on the journey of the Self. You have the will and the right to experience what you desire without interference. But there is a catch—you can only experience what you acknowledge to be true at any given moment. Complete knowledge and truth are housed in every cell of your body, but it is up to you to break out of limit and seek to know what you cannot yet imagine.

Some of you have never fit comfortably in your life but have lived only to expand the Self view. It's not always an easy thing to do when you are the only one dancing to the tune of Self exploration. In order to survive, you may find it easier to gather together with those who are of like mind. I encourage you to continue to explore, with great courage, the journey of all possibility and truth, and to experience the wonders that await you. Remember to love and respect those who don't choose to live as you do. You are the only one who can change and grow your unique spark from Original Thought, which is the Self of your being. Come forth into the act of being and believe in the Self. There is nothing else that matters.

Now, let us once more delve into the conscious and unconscious minds in order to resolve the conflict that runs through mankind as it seeks a path to enlightenment. In truth, there is no such thing as two minds. Nor is there a golden ring one must catch called "enlightenment." The term "enlightenment" is really just another name for journey. Throughout time, many master teachers have spoken of the path to enlightenment at great length. At one time or another, you may have sat at the feet of such a master in total absorption and agreement with the teachings. Sit there if you choose, but remember to always think for yourself. It is actually not possible to truly enlighten, for it implies that you are not already who I know you to be. I have told you that the entirety of the universal order is alive in every cell of your body. You are Original Thought personified. The truth of these teachings may be difficult to comprehend when you are continually bombarded with outside interference. But you are now, and always have been, enlightened beings. You are one mind, one body, one purpose and one Spirit-Soul in human form. What a blessing it is to gaze upon you! You are adventurers, seekers of experience, pathfinders, road builders, doers and shakers. And you are gods.

The idea of enlightenment is a lofty one and has often been presented as the ultimate accomplishment. You have been told that by following the dictates of this teacher or that particular religion, spiritual belief or ancient text, you will be able to achieve, if you are very, very good, a certain level of enlightenment. I would tell you, and have told you repeatedly, that you already have all this knowledge and are enlightened right now. It is interesting to watch you search for answers—praying and waiting for that seemingly illusive transformation into enlightenment— when you already possess the thing that you seek. True enlightenment has been yours from the beginning of your spark. Look around you and see what you have created from your journey this time around. Some will look and be pleased that they are well-fed, happy, loved and richly clothed. Others will look at their life and say "I am not pleased. I am sick, I am not loved, I have hateful thoughts and I am treated poorly. I lack, I lack, I lack." Is one human journey better than another, one human more deserving than another? No, of course not. These journeys may seem painfully different, but they are still the human journey of enlightened beings. How could it be anything else? If everything is contained in each cell that makes up the very form that you are, how can one be lacking and one more deserving? These are the same cells, the same birth and the same Original Thought personified. But the outcome of each journey depends on the level of evolved truth the Spirit-Soul possesses at the time of birth.

In this particular expression of life on your planet, there is a belief in opposites. I have spoken of this before. If there is good, there has to be the counterbalance of evil. If there is black, there must be white. Up is heaven, down is hell. Opposites. Where there is life, there is also death. Opposites. You are journeying on a planet that is comprised of created opposites, and you have come here for the purpose of experiencing these opposites. This was your choice. There are planets where opposites do not exist. There are civilizations that live out the truth of their Original Thought purpose without conflict. Yours is not one of them. What is being attempted on your planet, after billions of years of experimentation, is a journey back to the beginning where enlightenment of the Spirit-Soul simply *Is*—complete unto itself. Look to the Self, for it is yet another journey you travel. The ability to create and the free will to journey as you choose are all part of being enlightened. Try to live the wisdom you have been given—if only for a moment in your busy, busy day—and begin to reap the benefits of your discovery.

CHAPTER TWENTY-TWO

# COMMUNION

Meditation and prayer are the practices of speaking and being with the Self and your God. Whether you sit and breathe in silence, look to the heavens, kneel, bow or touch your head to the ground in reverence, your purpose is to find peace and communion with your God. You may follow certain rituals in order to achieve this union, but in the end it really doesn't matter, for the goal is the same: your communion with the God/Self through contemplation. If your mind becomes filled with fleeting thoughts and random pictures when you first sit in silent union, do not despair. This is part of the process that allows you to sift through what is truly important to the Self, and it helps to cleanse the human mind of all attachments. When you are free from interference and can sit with the Self in peaceful silence, your communion with truth has begun.

There are spiritual teachers who teach their followers how they must pray and meditate. In some cases they describe how you must approach this silent union, what words to recite, and how to use the breath and the correct positioning of the body for complete supplication. For the novice seeker, these instructions are helpful in the beginning, but eventually you learn that true communion is achieved when you do what feels right for you. I have seen some of you achieve this state of silent communion working in your garden, while in a room full of people, or simply when listening to beautiful music. This union can be achieved by allowing the time and space in which to embrace the True Mind experience. It may be helpful to use words from your heart to express and set your desired focus:

*I am completely aware and at One with my God.*

*We are One.*

*My heart is open to receive only the highest light.*

*I am surrounded by your love, and I am All life contained in a single cell.*

I hesitate to even give these examples, for I wish you to be completely in tune with your unique Self and not with the truth as seen through my eyes. Full recognition and acceptance of the Self as God in the body human and the one True Self can be accomplished through meditation/prayer. When you are in True Mind, you are the True Self without separation. Be the observer of your thought patterns throughout each day and you will gain great insight. When one is the constant observer without judgment, accessing the Self through meditation, the meditative state becomes one continuous focus. Through meditation/prayer you learn to access the Self more readily, as opposed to living the duality of human experience. Only then the True Self becomes the proper noun for who you are in truth.

To live the life of a human is a wonderful gift, but trying to reach the human who is completely absorbed in experiencing conscious existence is like knocking on a door that is never opened. Mankind, do not stand behind this door of ignorance any longer. There is no need. Many of us have come to gain entrance, expand your spiritual awareness and seed the ground for your awakening. It has always been the belief on this planet that in order to exist as human you must live within certain parameters. Many of you fear what lies beyond these barriers. Meditation silences the human consciousness, allows access to these barriers and helps to calm your fears.

When you live within the meditative experience, you begin to step in and out of limit. You are being challenged to expand your conscious mind and to accept new revelations from the True Mind perspective. Contrary to popular belief, you are not being asked to transcend your human body to become the All in a flash of insight and blinding light. Instead, what we are attempting to develop is your unrealized potential while still in the human body. This is the challenge of humankind. If you were simply beamed up as is, what would be the point?

Some of the wisdom that has been shared is ancient, but it is part of the All that has lived in the cells of your body from the beginning. This truth never changes. These cells are the basic building blocks of all creation and correspond to Original Thought's intention. Be the observer of what is occurring in your life and what you have placed into your box of limits in order to survive. I am not asking you to transcend your human body. Why would you, when you already contain it All? What you transcend is "limit." I am asking you to use this knowledge to gain wisdom, create at will and be in peace. If you are not in peace, you are not observing your life clearly. If you don't like what you see, then change it through your creative will. The only way in which to truly transcend ignorance is to be conscious and aware every step of the way by embracing wisdom and truth.

There is truly no separation and never has been. When my scribe sits with me and says her prayer to be a clear and open channel through which information and truth will flow, this prayer contradicts her understanding and acceptance of this very truth. If what she receives is not part of who she truly is, then she would merely be a hollow tube through which information is poured. When you begin to accept and understand a truth such as this, it opens the door to the exploration of further possibilities. Your expanding awareness and acceptance of the All as contained in one tiny cell—really just a speck of matter—is constant. I only bring to your attention what is already seeded in your cellular memory. The question now is how you can begin to access this knowledge and live it as truth. The higher God Self does not sit outside you somewhere in the heavens; this all-knowing God Self is fully functional and contained within your human form from inception. To be sure, you are made up of blood and bones and various body parts, but you are also a product of the smallest unit of life giving force—the universal cell.

If the All that has ever been is contained in each cell, then what is it that you seek? I believe you seek the awareness and full realization of what is contained within this cell. Am I correct? The meditations, the chanting, the praying and the seeking of wisdom at the feet of a guru are all attempts to connect to this knowledge. There is nothing wrong with seeking wisdom in this way, but, in truth, what you seek outside the Self is never enough. You walk around with a half-empty cup that is never completely filled as you continue to search. It is the way of the earthbound human. I do not reproach you for this seeking because it has brought you here, but I would have you keep an open mind and be willing to release old concepts and embrace even older ones. Confusing, is it not? The pure lights who began this planet never conceived the possibility that you would forget your brilliance and connection to the All in the process of experimentation and adventure. But what developed over time was the belief that in order to survive, certain adjustments had to be made. As a result, a more solid human form evolved which soon was made to accept limitation and opposites within the kingdom of the one True Self.

It is time once more to acknowledge the universal cell, which is your beginning spark and the pulsating life force that surrounds the human form in complete truth and connection to Original Thought. You are within this womb of creation, while possessing the ability to create simultaneously. Observe the many layers of experience that make up your reality. Then move beyond what has been your truth and seek connection from a loftier perspective. You created this scenario. Now live it as you have dictated, and be in joy for your absolute brilliance. The messages that have been translated by my scribe are ones in which many truths are told and many levels of deceit are revealed. The word "deceit" may have more of an evil connotation than is intended but is still meant in the strictest sense. The deceit and lies that have been imposed upon humanity over time were not originally intended for evil purpose. These lies were motivated by individuals who thought of themselves as altruistic and kind and who believed these religious stories and spiritual messages would afford the masses a focus for worship. The faithful soon learned that it was far easier to have the support and camaraderie found in the religious communities of the day than to go against the norm.

The stories that were told in the various religious texts were well-intentioned and a way in which to unite the people toward a common cause or belief system. They were most often about good triumphing over evil and were accepted as truth. There were gods, fairies and other worldly creatures to fill out the theme and keep the audience enchanted. There was magic and mystery, and usually a supreme, all-knowing, fierce or benevolent god overseeing it all. The people were judged, freed or condemned by the whim of this god. Atrocities were committed in the god's name. Arrogance and righteousness were proclaimed by whoever carried the biggest stick. From the first telling, those who built a base of followers through these stories of old—be they king, priest, shaman or shepherd—determined your history. Was it all based on lies? Most of it was, but it became truth when enough of you were willing to focus upon it and make it so in your conscious mind. So, here you are, not knowing what may be truth and what may be fiction, contemplating the possibility that what you have believed is suddenly in fear of crumbling. How will you know what to reject and what to trust? Are you listening to yet another fairytale by one who wishes to deceive? If you can question at all, then your True Mind is in operation and you are ready to listen from yet another perspective. That is all I ask. I want you simply to consider that the foundation you have been standing on may have many flaws. I want you to open the mind a bit more and acknowledge what has been your truth so far.

I have spoken to you of Original Thought and that you are the spark from God that took human form to adventure and expand knowledge. Entering this limited state of existence, you embraced the belief in opposites and accepted restrictions that weren't necessarily part of who you were in truth. For billions of years, there have been storytellers, priests, shamans and teachers who have designated the parameters within which to live your life. Seeking unity and strength in numbers, the human took on these various belief systems and lived life within the dogma of the moment. Now you've listened to yet another called Mother, whose words are recorded through an innocent scribe in an attempt to lift the veils of deceit, and you wonder what to believe. Perhaps you feel out of balance, a little angry and confused. If so, this is a very good place to start.

Did Jesus die on the cross? Was there a Jesus? Did Buddha sit under that blessed tree and become illumed without so much as a bowl of rice? Did Moses part the seas? There are many stories, and through the telling they have become the facts around which you built your life. For the most part, these stories have done no harm, but many of them have been the justification for wars and atrocities throughout history. Though the original intent was to bring groups of like-minded people together for the sake of safety and unity of purpose, this was often usurped by dogma that was meant to control. You may find yourself in a dilemma of sorts as you continue to read and listen to yet one more story—the one I bring; the one I call "truth." I ask only that you listen and then decide for yourself. Take your time and discount or accept what resonates as truth for you. Many of you continue to find great comfort in your churches, synagogues, temples and other places of worship, and I do not attempt to take this peace from you. Simply contemplate the possibility that the truth I bring may expand your adventure of exploration and bring a richer perspective.

This new adventure will not bring you home, as some of you believe, but may allow you to view your life more from a place of forgiveness and truth than one of judgment. You are already home. Your home is the Self.

# CHAPTER TWENTY-THREE

# WHAT IS AND WHAT CAN BE

Throughout time, great masters have had one primary goal: to teach truth and bring mankind into the knowledge and acceptance of the Self as revealed within this truth. But religious dogma also gained acceptance and resulted in many brutal wars waged in the erroneous belief that one truth was greater than the other. What if I were to tell you that everything that has ever been shared with humankind by every master who has ever stepped forward to espouse his truth is accurate? Would this understanding and acceptance bring an end to dissension? Perhaps it would, but more than likely it would not, as human consciousness allows for freedom of choice in such matters. You have only to watch your news programs and read your history to see that this is an accurate observation. Truth is indeed in the eye of the beholder. The Self selects what fits a desired life experience and then lives that experience. One truth is not greater than another but merely a blip on your screen of wisdom gained. As you continue to operate within the belief of opposites here on your planet, you may see your experiences as either good or bad. You make choices based on this experience and, if you are very, very clever, you continue your forward momentum.

I have brought you teachings from ancient times, and, for each of you, there resonates a response totally unique to the Self, that cannot be measured or judged by anyone as to its validity. You are learning to recognize the Self when presented through the experience of forward motion. The seeker must always move forward and reach for that illusive brass ring. When you finally grasp the ring of eternal knowledge, what will you do then? Will you sit back and say, "Now I can rest"? Perhaps you have been resting all along. Some have called this place of rest "sleep." Some have called it "reincarnation." Some have not called it by any name because they don't recognize what is happening to them from one moment to the next. We call this "sleepwalking" through life. But you know now, don't you? You have called the truth forth, so it is being revealed unto you. Truth is revealed when the seeker seeks to know.

When you are committed to finding truth at every turn, you continue on in a never ending cycle of experience. This experience leads you from the place of What Is into the eternal What Can Be, as you move through many levels of expanded awareness. Your journey is without end through the path of infinity. The recognized symbol for infinity appears as an elongated figure eight resting on its side, connected and woven together in an unbroken line. But this symbol could more accurately depict reincarnation and the cycle of sameness in an ongoing, unbroken line. The infinity sign would more accurately symbolize all possibility and truth if, in its place, the final line was broken open and allowed to stretch forward into forever. As True Mind emerges and expands, further knowledge is revealed. Never remaining static, you continue moving and waiting for the final truth to be revealed. What I have attempted to teach you is that there is no final truth to be sought or a golden key that will unlock the complete answer. Creation does not stand still and is always changing and evolving. If you accept this truth, how can there be a final answer when there is no "final" to be found? To be sure, you are travelers and seekers of knowledge, but you may rest on whatever truth suits your purpose at any time in the continuum, until you wake to yet another possibility and begin the search again. Be the ever-vigilant observer of your current beliefs and then move more into the realm of "what if." Make this choice freely and you will experience the difference it makes in your life. To "know" is to cognize at a higher level than simply understanding through the human consciousness. True creation is knowing when you hear something that is true and then beginning to act upon this truth.

Mankind is the creator of the here and now. There is no finer example of this than when my scribe would come each morning before dawn to write messages from a source that could not be seen or heard with the human senses. She wrote these messages from the place of knowing, and trusted that what was recorded was from a higher source. I would often ask her,

"What if this higher source is you? What if this knowing that you attend to most diligently comes from All That You Are in truth? Would it make what you record any less powerful? Would the material presented be any less viable and true? What if this knowing is simply the act of accessing All That You Are in totality?" Mankind doesn't know this to be true, so my scribe has agreed to connect to one who will guide her through these realizations and discovery and then share them with others. Embrace this act of knowing, and allow full access to the realms waiting to be acknowledged.

In observing your world and being witness to a variety of life events, you have experienced a wide range of emotions that make up the human conscious expression. You have walked through the minefield of doubt and despair and come out the other side unscathed. In short, you have been experiencing what you created from the place of Original Thought. Ask yourself: *Was it the intention of Original Thought to bring pain to this planet, as well as joy?* As you are that spark from Original Thought and given free will to create your journey, what have you done with the privilege this opportunity affords? It always comes back to the Self. You have free will to create from the place of Original Thought but may need to examine what this truly means. Do not waste your time in judgment of any past or present creations, but always be aware of what is possible as you move toward the future. It is up to you to review and judge your creations, not I. If you can do this from the heart and with an open mind, you are ready to create the present and the forever more from truth. From the beginning of the thought that was you, creation has been yours to command. Sparks from Original Thought forming and merging within the unformed primordial space began their journey as "creators."

Now you have awakened to find yourself within a confined box that has numerous rules and set beliefs. Many outside factions and unrestrained religious dogma have attempted—and succeeded, in most cases—to restrict your journey and harness your innate power. Know this: you have never lost the ability to return to the time of Original Thought creation and change what you wish at any time. "You create your own reality" is a nice, tidy statement that doesn't really tell you much at all. If anything, it may lead you to believe you are somehow a failure if you don't create that beautiful house, new life or a love you may feel is your ultimate goal.

The assumption that you can create easily from your current mindset of limitation is inaccurate, for you cannot create anything but further limit. It is not a failure on your part but simply a lack of understanding of the process. So, you might ask, what is the process of creating what you want? First, recognize the True Mind fully and then continue searching for ways to create by being the observer of your present life and building your roadmap to creation.

When you were the newly minted, bright and shiny sparks of Original Thought, you created with ease. This was your right, and a wonderful adventure. But now, when you live with judgment and within a limited mindset, it is more difficult, but still not impossible, to remember and embrace this knowing without some outside assistance. And this is where I come in. Yes, I am an entity unto myself, but you have called me forth from your creative power to bring an understanding that has been lost for a very long time. It is time to acknowledge your God-given power and create what you will. In the process, you may find that what you thought were your most ardent desires are nothing more than fantasy as you create in earnest from new truth

I have led you through many openings in spirit to a level of understanding you have just begun to access. Your conscious mind is still not operating fully when you fail to recognize the True Mind as your vehicle through the obstacles of judgment. But you are learning and, in the process, embracing many insights and truths. The way of a creative being is never to be stagnant but always searching for more. This force is voracious and fully operating within you right now. Do not ask me for a roadmap to follow and create from True Mind or to determine how this will occur for you. When I ask you to be the observer, you are given the opportunity to build your own roadmap so that you may clearly see the bumps in the road that have prevented you from creating what you want. Why do I ask you to be the observer? Is it to judge what you have done or have become? That would be a waste of my time, and most certainly a waste of yours.

When you build your own roadmap of creation, you are allowing that spark of Original Thought, the uniqueness that is you, to come forth. Creation is never static but always moving and forming from the thoughts of the True Mind currently in full operation. You have always created from the place of True Mind because, in reality, there has never been a separation. By viewing the result of your former creations called "the life that you lead," you will understand what your thought processes have been and, from this observation, gain powerful insight and wisdom as you continue your forward momentum. Contemplate what has been given so far. Be the observer of who you are in this world and create consciously from the True Mind experience.

Releasing mankind from the fear that has kept it living within the status quo of limited beliefs is an adventure in and of itself. Replacing what you once believed to be true with something new can be life-changing. I speak of more than your life on terra; I speak of your universal life, the one that you were first birthed to experience. This is the life to which you strive to return. And if that is truly the case, you might rightfully ask, "Why do we leave such perfection in the first place?" This is a good question, and I believe I have given you the answer many times before. Some sparks from Original Thought have been content to never travel far from the Source, though "far" in the universal sense is still a rather long trip. When your first spark came into existence, some of you decided to expand and create worlds of your own to explore. When we came to the caves of learning, it was to seek just this kind of adventurous exploration. At any given moment, a journey can be transformed if there is a willingness to expand beyond perceived limits. This is not to imply that you actually have limits. Quite the contrary. But these are the beliefs you willingly accepted to journey as a human on this planet. At times I feel much like an archeologist, sifting through the layers of accumulated dust and debris of the human norm, removing each layer until your truth is fully uncovered. Mankind, you are on an adventure, a treasure hunt to root out the beliefs that have kept you bound and experiencing limits that were never meant to hide the truth.

Housed in the cranium of the entity called "human," the brain has hidden within its depths another layer of potential, waiting to be discovered. In keeping with the rhetoric of our previous headings, I am tempted to call it the True Brain, but that would seem a little too commonplace for what it really is. This microscopic core brain is very similar to a computer chip that is accessible at any time. To understand it, you first have to believe that it is there in reality, if not actual substance, in order to experience its unlimited powers. I say "if not actual substance" because you won't find it with any of your X-ray machines. The visible, monster brain that fills your cranium was originally formed to cover and protect the microscopic core brain, much like the casing that surrounds the hard drive on a computer. Through the process of evolution, this monster brain grew and the existence of the True Brain was quickly forgotten. When my scribe receives and records these messages, she is actually operating out of this mini-brain, microchip base. She was told that she inherited the information she recorded every day, and that is a fairly accurate description. Access to the database of the All is in this mini-brain storehouse.

Don't bother looking for this microchip-sized brain on the physical level because it is an analogy to illustrate a point. What is the point? You do not operate out of the monster brain for anything other than human survival on your planet. What you are being asked to do is accept the *idea* of connection to the Source of All wisdom and truth and know you have this innate ability already. I thought this was a good way to gain your attention and make this point. If you have access to all the information in the universal order, why don't you use it? Good question. The mini-brain is an illustrated connection of what might happen when you take a step out of limit and explore other possibilities. Some of you are already making those shifts while stepping outside limit and allowing your journey of all possibility to continue.

Blessed be the seeker of wisdom. Blessed be the one who knows. Blessed be the truth of all creation, for it is you. It is you. It is you. Create from this space of all knowing, and find joy in your discoveries.

# CHAPTER TWENTY-FOUR

# THE NEW EARTH

Mankind is in the process of awakening the temporal lobe and the mini-microchip of the inner brain to full capacity. As a result, subtle changes and shifts in consciousness have begun to occur in your life as you move forward on the time continuum. This is one of the most important reasons for new information to be brought forth in the twenty-first century. Some of you are experiencing delightful, confusing and often amazing events in your life, and have used these experiences to acknowledge and further your adventure in timelessness. There are those who remember the beginning, when your planet was still forming, for they have that memory embedded within their cellular structure. This memory has brought them back to this land for another experience and a reunion of like souls, who will gather together to communicate and learn what they must in this adventure called "life's journey." Rotating around the sun, your earth is fast coming to a time when the current resources used to sustain life are being depleted, while new ones are being discovered. The sun will still shine, the rain will continue to fall and the wheels of modern man will forever turn. Why wouldn't they? Your scientists will continue research into alternative fuels and discover new energy sources that change the way in which you live. These investigations have already begun. You will harness the sun, and its rays will be stored and transformed into clean, clear energy on a more global scale. Your scientists will discover how to break down the sun's rays into subatomic particles, combine them with atoms and add a presently unknown source of energy from the earth's core to produce a product that is clean, constant and free. You have all the elements available to you now, and your scientists are diligently working to unlock the secret of these yet unknown energy sources and make them free for public consumption.

A few world leaders and some ordinary citizens are using their influence to change the world for the better. They may be ridiculed at times but remain earnest in their mission to continue in spite of any censure. Many positive changes are occurring throughout the world, some of which you may read about in your news. I have given you a little preview of what is to come so you may know that the timing of these messages is consistent with the evolutionary process of your planet. For those who see the world destroying itself, please reconsider your negative thoughts. Join with those who are committed to the continued growth and adventure that was your gift from the inception of the universal order. Countless numbers have returned to this planet now for just this purpose—to see that this experiment in creation continues. Some are the very scientists who will be making these discoveries. Many of these scientists will gain further insight by tapping into the flow of information and energy that is always available in the universal river of knowledge.

The principle motivation of the movers and shakers of your planet is to see the world continue to prosper and thrive. They are peace-loving, unselfish and devoted to this cause. It is why they have come. I see these beings for who they are—returning Spirit-Souls whose journey and purpose is for the betterment and peace of the universe as a whole. The shifting focus of the world's governments toward the good of all mankind will allow these discoveries to come to fruition, and all will be as intended for purposeful good. So many discoveries will occur that you will find it a most pleasant place in which to live out your journey. As the people who have come for just this purpose begin to tap into this universal flow of ideas and present them in a form that can be useful, there will be significant changes for the better. The influx of new ideas for the advancement of humanity will be uppermost in the minds of all mankind, and a new dawn of pure thought and undiluted truth will be the result. That is what you have been waiting and preparing for, and the time is now upon you. Will there be wars? Probably. Will there be sickness and crimes against humanity? More than likely. Enlightenment is a process that takes time and attention to evolve. The purpose of that process is to gain the wisdom and knowledge that you will always have a place from which to choose truth, to seek peace and joy and to realize happiness. This understanding is embedded within the Spirit-Soul and will continue to grow and be refined. You are perfect as you were created, for creation is not static but fluid, and you are forever in the process of expanding. There is hope for the future of this planet, this emerald of the Universe. Take heart in the realization that you are here during this time of awakening. Tap into that universal flow of information available to assist you as you move throughout your day.

Hopefully by now you have come to learn that the journey of the Self is your true path. *Come forth into the act of being and believe in the Self* was your first initiation into the importance of the Self. Coming forth, as you do each day, into the act of being is a transformational journey. Each dawn you awaken to a new opportunity, a new commitment to become the observer of what gives your life meaning. To be the observer is to understand that you are looking at not only what is visible on the outside but what is felt on the inside as well. It is important to realize that how you react and appear to the world is often dependent upon the circumstances that surround you. As you adapt to fit into each situation, you smile at the right time, are polite to others and speak half-truths when you deem them necessary. The Self has the ability to focus in a multitude of places at once while continuing to express without pause. The expanded potential of the True Self to experience in the universal order has no limit.

There may be times on your journey of the Self when you feel the need to sleep more. Maybe some days you're a little clumsier or generally feel out of sorts with the world. You'll be glad to know it is during these times you are most often going through an important transformational processes of expanding Spirit-Self. At times like these, take care of your body, rest and stay safe while you balance what is being given from Source with what you currently believe. When you are asked to step outside your box of limits, it is for the purpose of integrating these opportunities into your present reality. It is important that you have a conscious understanding of this process so that fear is not the overriding factor as you begin to more fully explore the Self. Every moment that you spend with this material is an opportunity for growth. Often the words you read are less important than what is simultaneously occurring within the cells of your body and in your expanding brain as it makes connections to further realizations.

Find your peace in the knowledge that you are evolving in perfection as you continue your journey forward.

Each of you is unique. There is no single roadmap to follow—only the one that you create for your journey. Any information you are given along the way is simply to assist you on the path you choose to follow. There is no right or wrong way to attain the recognition and acceptance of the Self. Do not deny what you know to be true or look to another for your truth. Seek camaraderie and companionship along the way, but keep to your own truth. Who did Buddha seek to know when he sat in contemplation? No one, save the Self. If you bow down to Buddha's likeness or kneel in front of Jesus on the cross, remember to honor the journey of the Self that each of them took to gain and share great wisdom. The possibilities of any journey are as vast and exceptional as each spark from Original Thought. Where will you place your focus today? This is a good thing to ask yourself, for where you focus will determine your day and the events that surround you. You are that powerful. There is a popular saying on your planet: "Create your day." This is a significant teaching. How will you apply it to what you have learned so far? Be at peace, for the sun shines within you. Do not always look for it outside the Self.

The Self, expressed as human, has cloaked itself in limited thought and continues to do so as mankind repeats the process of reincarnation. There are some rewards to being in human form, and most never want anything else. It is not to those humans I speak. In order to move forward, you must come to the place of willing separation from the limits of human form and possess a searching attitude and a sincere desire for knowledge of a more spiritual nature. I say "of a more spiritual nature" because it is within the *nature of Spirit* that one relinquishes the limit of sensory experience and reaches out to touch what has been forgotten. Faith in the unknown and unseen is part of any spiritual quest and is present in those who worship and believe in a Supreme God. This God is called by many names and prayed to in a ritualized format with rules that have been set down by man. But within those parameters there may be little opportunity for an expanded journey of adventure to begin in earnest.

In ancient and unrecorded times on your planet, and in galaxies much older than yours, the search for the Self has never been the focus. Life was filled to capacity with single-minded awareness of the Self as wholly connected to God/Source, the Spirit-Soul of your Being. Now, because much has been forgotten, many spiritual teachers have come to your planet to heed the call from those who desire to know more and to remember the Self. *Once you recognize that you are an expression of the Self, you are the closest you can ever be to Original Thought and still be earthbound in human form.* This connection is inherent in every cell of your body. To access this connection is to acknowledge that there may be more to life than what you are currently experiencing. You read, you think, you pray, you explore and you talk with like-minded people, as well as those that you love. Why do I say that you should talk with those that you love, your family, friends and colleagues? Simply because these are the people you have created to experience within your current sphere of reality. They fit within the spaces you have provided and have insights to teach you about yourself that you can get from no other source.

I am forever asking you to be the observer. You may go back into the past and relive every little detail if you wish, but it's not necessary for your evolution—though there are many self-help tools that give you that opportunity. Make it easy on yourself. Simply look at the realities of your life, acknowledge the life you have created and your current beliefs, and be willing and eager to expand beyond them.

The Self is an all-encompassing Spirit-Soul. It is not only your aeroship but who you are—unique unto any other life form. The Self is the reflection, the reminder, the mirror of it All. Gaze into the Self and envision with eyes that cannot see. Listen for the words that are spoken but cannot be heard with the human ear. Feel the difference between being in the expanded presence of the Self and living within your box of limit. The Self is expansive in nature and cannot be contained. The Self always moves in a forward motion. You are the Self personified. I can hear the questions ticking away in your mind: *So, why am I not fully conscious and operating within the Self now?* I will tell you this: you are operating within the Self now and have been from the beginning. The memory of any form you have ever created to experience and adventure has always been fully contained within the Self. The Self is revealed to you in many ways, so I ask you once again to be the observer of your life. Manifest what you desire and then observe the results. Do you see clearly through the eyes of one who has connection to the All? Do you walk with purpose upon this planet? Do you have purpose? Take the time to contemplate what has been given and how you wish your life to evolve from this time forward.

Many of you are rapidly approaching a crossroad and experiencing an evolution of ideas and beliefs, dogma and truth. It is an invigorating place to be on your path of expanding consciousness. As your journey continues, your interests and priorities may change, though you remain tied to the outcome of your actions. How is it possible to evolve spiritually and still survive the onslaught of emotions that are part of life on your planet? When one is in the place of expansion and able to see certain truths clearly, then the negative outcomes associated with emotions such as hatred, fear, greed and guilt are obvious. While, at times, these outcomes may seem hopeless to overcome, it is not impossible and is entirely within your capabilities to do so. You are experiencing that process now. Expanding your conscious awareness needn't be painful, but it will always be thought-provoking. How you handle it is entirely up to you. It is my intention to assist you in the recognition of what is occurring and support you in your process.

Mankind, you are deeply invested in your human life. Not many of you live on a mountaintop in quiet contemplation, meditating on the all-encompassing One. Nor do you reside in a monastery or spiritual retreat. Instead, you are completely immersed in human emotions and the drama of everyday life. The contemplation of more spiritual matters is rarely a priority. While living her life, my scribe continued to rise every morning to greet her day and record these missives. During this process, she was often distracted and unsure of how to proceed but did so anyway. And as I have stated before, this is one of the keys to the evolutionary process. *You must always continue to move forward.* It is as simple as that. All that surrounds you at any given moment, on any given day and in any form or circumstance is but a fleeting blip on the screen of your forward momentum. It is better to be determined to live your life consciously in constant movement and exploration.

When you find yourself at a crossroad, do you seek peace in what is familiar, or search for the esoteric and spiritual beauty of the soul? I encourage you to keep to the path of evolutionary truth and trust it to lead you back to Original Thought personified. Have faith that what is given unto you is valid and worth the effort. This is not a judgment of your life but an observation of what boundaries continue to live in the mind of man. Accept this opportunity to suspend judgment and limit and embrace the expansion of your mind. Is all judgment limited? Most certainly. But it is important to learn the lesson that judgment teaches if truth is ever to be completely understood. Be the observer. Step outside these limited parameters and view your judgments with a deeper understanding and clarity. Do I want you to take a very long time in dissecting your judgments? No. Simply be the observer, learn what you will and keep moving forward.

The River of Life, known as the Nile, is the longest river in the world. In this river is plant and animal life that has existed since the birth of humans upon your planet. Within this river flow the annals of time. The tributaries formed from this river of timelessness anoint many lands. As the waters are taken up and dispensed once more as rain, this mighty river touches everything that has ever been and everything that shall ever be upon your planet. It is that grand and that important. All this from just one ancient source.

I have used the river Nile as an analogy to represent Original Thought and the far-reaching effect of the One that is embraced by the All, of which we are a part. There are those among you who wonder how the All could have possibly evolved from the One, and you are told to have faith. Usually when you are told to have faith, it's because a reasonable explanation cannot be made for what you are asked to believe. So I used the river as an analogy for the connection that we have to Source, which touches and is a part of everything, and asked you to have faith in the process of the transformation that awaits you. You are entering a time when faith just might have to be enough for now until you begin to fully understand who you are. Truth has but one source and there is no other. That source is the One. When you are in doubt, remember the Nile and the effect one river can have on everything it touches. Life perpetuates life. Truth perpetuates truth. It is an ongoing cycle that has existed from the beginning. *You are more the river than you are the human.* You have only to look at the ratio of water in your body in relation to all else and you will know of what I speak.

When I ask you to be the observer of your life, it may be helpful for you to know it is something I continue to practice. I have gained a good deal of insight and wisdom from observing the actions and reactions of my scribe, as well as the inner workings of her mind. When she ponders her purpose, I say "It is to continue." And for all of you it is the same. Your purpose can be as simple or as complex as you desire, depending on what you wish to experience. The willingness of anyone steeped in human life to find a quiet place and silence the mind to receive is magnificent for me to behold. It is good for you to know that in this goal- oriented world of yours, you often forget that the process is as important as the outcome. Find a quiet place in your day to open the mind to new truth and reap the rewards of your search. Seek truth in all that surrounds you. Be as the river—ancient, yet moving and teeming with life-force—and find your peace.

I have given you the opportunity to gain wisdom and grow the Self in the process. This is how a student becomes a teacher. What awaits you is a great deal more exciting than you can imagine. Faith can be a consequence of challenge, and I challenge you to continue on. As a result, what enters into and falls away from your life will be timely. Remember to be at peace, for this is one of the most important teachings I have given you so far. The truth is always simple. The truth survives as you continue. Greet each day with a renewed spirit, and be at peace. Always, always choose peace.

# CHAPTER TWENTY-FIVE

# WHAT IS THE SELF?

In the course of a human lifetime, it is believed that there are always valleys to cross, rivers to forge and mountains to climb. As you continue moving forward on your journey, you begin to discover and remove certain beliefs that no longer serve you. Some of them have been with you for lifetimes. The brief lifespan of the body is one belief that mankind has manifested, as demonstrated in the ongoing cycle of birth, death and, for some who acknowledge this, rebirth.

Now consider this possibility. What if you could simply appear as a fully-formed child or adult human whenever and wherever you wish to have a life experience and then simply move on when the lesson was done? It would be like attending a class one period of the day to learn the lesson presented and then leaving when the bell rings, the period ends and your life experience is complete. Some of you are actually doing this now but are not aware it is happening. What if this is how you have always lived life? Have you become so enmeshed in the cyclical adventure of birth and death on your planet that you have forgotten your ability to leave the body at will? My purpose is simply to seed this possibility into your conscious awareness for consideration. It is a good place to leave you—teetering on the cliff's edge of all possibility and gazing across to the other side for answers.

When you are alone with your thoughts, do you contemplate your life as a human entity? Do you look back to what has been and then forward to what shall be written in your future? By doing so, you allow a deeper experience of life's journey. Contemplating only your day-to-day existence without reference to past events would find you living while only partially awake. The past is as much a part of you as your present existence. It is this combination of both past and present experience that leads to the successful resolution of your choices in life. You accept that there is a *now;* you acknowledge that there has been a *past* and you exist within this frame of reference. Expand your mind a bit more to take in what I am attempting to teach you. It is that important. I have told you truths. I have not embellished half-truths or cultivated lies. Nor have I asked you to accept any misconceptions in an attempt to control and manipulate you. I wish you to continue to stretch your mind a little more and find the point of human existence through the contemplation of past and future actions. Where would you be without a past? What would you seek if you could not move toward the future? Would you exist at all? Perhaps it is time to contemplate your existence as more than just a human entity or even that of a Spirit-Soul.

There are Masters who have taught you to focus the breath and the mind in meditation and prayer to achieve a specific purpose. What is it you seek when you meditate or pray? Is it a release from pain? Is it a roadmap for future times or a deeper understanding of your purpose? We have talked about the adventure of exploration, moving toward the wellspring of knowledge and living life fully. Is this all you want? It may well be for awhile. In the course of a lifetime, you may explore one belief system or another as you search for answers. But somewhere along the way, if you have been paying really close attention, you may begin to realize that a human life may not be all you seek to know and you begin to search a little more. You may start by reading books by great masters and attending their lectures. Or you may decide to visit a religious house of worship or learn a new way of meditating. There are so many opportunities to choose from that you neglect the very vehicle that is always available to you—the vehicle called the Self. What has the Self got to do with any of this seeking? It is the central core of your search and encompasses all the books, the lectures, the meditations and the religious belief systems you have ever explored. The Self brings you to a deeper understanding of why you are what you are and the purpose of your existence. You are that spark, the Self of Original Thought personified and cognized into lifetimes of experience that make up past and future reference. The Self oversees and is part of everything. It is the reason and the result all tied up in a single, unique bow.

When one speaks of the Self and the wisdom within, he is beginning to contemplate and understand *purpose*. The Self is revolutionary and alive with Spirit. It is the Spirit-Soul that fuels your motion. The Self will take you to places you can only imagine because they have yet to be created. The Self creates and is a living, striving and exuberant force. Pulsing with life, the Self builds a bridge of understanding between the human life form and Original Thought, the creator. This bridge of understanding is crossed by anyone who seeks to adventure. The ones you have called "saints" have, in their lifetime, crossed over this bridge and back into Original Thought while still within human form. Accessing this bridge of the Self brings forth the highest accomplishments of mankind. The Self as your aeroship takes you between the two seemingly opposite realities of past and future reference and into the realm of all possibility. As grandiose as it may seem, The Self is, in reality, the simplest of creation birthed from Original Thought. From this swirling mass have come the ideas, contemplations and your adventurous Spirit-Soul to journey. The search for the Self has been the goal of everything you have ever done or will do, now or in the future. The Self is just a word, but a word and a concept that says to the human who is seeking,

"I am the answer to your seeking. I am the answer to what it all means. I am the 'universal I' and, as such, will determine outcome."

You are all a part of the "universal I" and will find meaning in the Self. In the meantime, while this is occurring for you, you will be living past, present and future events and calling them "your life." You have opened a gate into the future contemplation of the Self. Reflect upon this and find your peace.

When one completely embraces the reality of the Self, a chemical reaction in your molecular structure takes place; something on par with alchemy. This seemingly magical process imbues the physical body with new energy focus. When one reaches such a stage of existence and has knowledge of certain undeniable truths, then one can move about multi-dimensional realities at will. And we've been reviewing such truths for you throughout these missives.

My scribe is one who has always accumulated much of her knowledge through her questing mind. Even as a child, in a lifetime we shared in the early days of Persia when we were together as teacher and student, she would ask and I would answer. My answers were often in the form of another question, which would then present further contemplation and questioning as our dialogues continued.

When mankind took on the cloak of forgetfulness and became incarnate beings embracing limit, you forgot to question. You readily accepted what was within your realm of experience as your only truth. While blind acceptance is important if you wish to maintain the status quo, stepping outside limit for even a brief moment allows expansion to occur. When one makes the commitment to live the life of an unlimited being for extended periods of time, he grows in wisdom and truth. And this is what I ask of you. Take a step outside and bathe yourself within this never-ending pool of light. Feel the energy of this expansion. Now create what you will. You have the ability. Why do you hesitate? Do you fear you will fail? Do you even know what you wish to create? The ability to create at will is comparable to winning the lottery. When you are suddenly given so much money, what do you do with these effortless winnings? What can you possibly buy enough of to make you happy? If you were to instantly realize and achieve the ability to create, travel to other dimensions or transcend your earthly connection, what would you do with all that you have been given?

You have journeyed within certain limited parameters all your life. Do you think these limits fall away with just one thought or one suggestion? No. Sorry to disappoint you, but it isn't always that easy. You formed these parameters for the purpose of experiencing life on this planet. These limitations have given you experiences that were not lived by those of us who first came to inhabit your planet. The seeds we planted within you were nurtured and left to germinate and bloom at will. As you begin to awaken to new wisdom you are often disappointed with your lack of ability to create. I understand. The lottery winner doesn't always find the joy that he thought would come from winning the prize money, and you haven't always found the answers you sought to create at will. The instantaneous awareness of the Self is not often possible here, though some have made claims to the contrary. Self-awareness is a process of unlocking the doors of limitation while working within the constraints of the seeker. Are you the seeker, or are you the lottery winner demanding instant satisfaction?

Come forth into the act of being and believe in the Self. Take a moment to lift the veil of forgetfulness and look upon the body that houses your Spirit-Soul. Everything you see within your world is "limit." This is not a judgment of who you are in this evolutionary process but an opportunity to further reveal the truth of limit. When you remove this veil from your mind and your body, what do you see? It may help in your contemplation to gaze into a mirror and look upon the physical manifestation that is reflected back. Think long and hard on the parts of you that are visible and the parts hidden within your limited form. Feel the beating of your heart—a wonderful mechanism that helps to sustain the body. Experience the life force carried by the blood pulsing through your veins. Lift the veil further and picture each cell, each atom of the body, engage the mind and become fully acquainted with the vehicle you brought to this place and time. You are simply a breathing, functioning human being on planet earth who is becoming acquainted with the Self, as fashioned by limit. Do you understand? You must first look deeply on your humanness and own these limits. Give yourself this gift of insight. Come forth into the act of being and believe in the Self—the one you have helped to create.

I encourage you to go slowly, take your time and find this seemingly elusive Self. It may please you to know that you can expand and experience all levels of existence while still within your present state of limitation. Everything is acceptable when in the midst of future exploration. The alchemist brings together different materials, respects the properties in each and combines them to produce wonderful creations. Can you not do the same? Allow the process of creation to unfold at the rate that will permit successful integration of your limits and the truth of the Self. The alchemist learns patience, and so will you. This is not an admonishment but a trust that is built between us. We are creating another way to exist within limitation. You may not fully understand that now, but you will. Let us continue and find the right combination together.

Locked within the hierarchy of the mind, and vital to human existence, is the complete knowledge of everything that has ever been and ever will be.

When one begins to access this knowing mind, it is a wonder to behold. Within this knowledge lies the answer to all life's questions. Imagine that. You have been walking around with the answers all this time. While searching through books, attending lectures and following the teachings of many Masters, the complete knowledge of who you are has been readily accessible from the beginning. All this time you have been looking *outside* the Self while the answers you sought have been waiting, unseen and unacknowledged, within your knowing mind.

You have been told that you were formed in perfection. Why, then, would your God leave you without complete knowledge? I use the term "your God" for those who may have a difficult time accepting the concept of Original Thought. To further your understanding and eliminate any stumbling blocks to the knowledge presented, you may call this God any name you wish. A great deal has been written of the conscious and the unconscious mind. I have suggested combining these two minds into the idea of one True Mind. Then, to further confuse the issue, I referred to the mind in such a way that negated the concept of True Mind all together. This was solely for the purpose of moving you past limits of any kind to allow further information and teachings to occur. While I will always attempt to eliminate your parameters, I am not above using them when necessary to move you forward.

Don't become weighed down by details, for they often interfere with greater wisdom and can slow the progress of the Spirit-Soul. When fully embracing the Spirit Mind, you have the opportunity to look at the sum total of your life experience. Take time to gaze into the universal mirror and contemplate this wisdom. Be the observer and stand outside the box of self-imposed rules more often. Only then will your Spirit-Soul be free to journey. When you attempt to soar from inside the box of limitations, you simply bump into walls and go around in circles. While still within this box of limitations, you may have read many books, listened to countless teachers, studied at the feet of gurus and worshiped in holy places. You have bounced around from place to place in your attempt to journey and often found the experiences discouraging. You may feel you've failed to grasp the highest meaning of your spiritual life, never once considering you were attempting to do so while living within limits. You begin to see the point.

Let us consider what occurs when sitting at the feet of a guru or any spiritual leader. What is gained from such devotion? You read the books and bow down to one ideal or another but never fully grasp what is seated before you. These priests, preachers, rabbis, mullahs and clerics of any and all belief systems are searching just as you are. There you sit, thinking they have all the answers, and they wait, hoping you will show them the answers. It is a mutual dependency that may need some revising to accomplish the purpose of your search. That purpose is how to live and journey to a deeper understanding of universal truth, while outside the box of limitation. When you journey outside limited perception, you are free to call your mind the conscious or unconscious and your Soul the Soul or Spirit-Soul... or a Twinkie for that matter. Outside the box of limitation, nothing matters except the realization that you are returning to that pure state of wonder, unlimited ability and adventure. What surrounds you now in your life can be viewed as an opportunity that will reverse the need to analyze, moralize or acknowledge anything that does not assist you to break free of limitation.

You don't have to disregard your job, your family or any part of your earthbound existence in order to adventure. That would be rather drastic and is simply not necessary—though there may be some who feel the need for a more sacrificial and dramatic away to achieve enlightened contemplation. You can break out of limit as I have taught you to do— within the walls of your home, surrounded by colleagues at work, walking on the beach or climbing a mountain; any place, any time, any way. If you think you have to do so in isolation, you are simply creating another limit for yourself. *Placing judgment on anything you choose to do puts you right back into your box of limits.*

Can you break down all barriers at once? Perhaps not right now, but be conscious of and pay attention to those moments of clarity and insight that come upon you. They may happen at any time, and you would be wise to reflect upon and integrate them into your Spirit-Soul existence. It doesn't matter how these moments of clarity come; simply honor them for what they bring and just keep moving. You will receive these insights more often when you are available and accepting. This is an important step in your journey and will remove boundaries and put you in the space of the unlimited thought patterns that are infused with infinite wisdom.

Allow these moments of clarity to evolve as they will. If you wish to gain further insight, write them down and read them over. Take your time. You are in the process of discovery. Experiencing and exploring this place of unlimited thought is a journey my scribe takes whenever we sit together. When she is able to step away from her boundaries and surrender, the messages come without hesitation. You live in a complicated world, but not so complicated that it can't be made simple at any given moment. For now, I would simply ask you to start with small steps. The end result is not really an end at all but only the beginning.

Take heart. Enjoy your life, and if you don't, change it. Make yourself available to the opportunities that exist. It matters not in the long run how you accomplish it. The most important thing is to continue. There is no stopping place and no quitting allowed. You are the creators of this opportunity for growth and insight. It is always you... always and ever the Self. On your journey, take time to enjoy the sun and the flowers and the rain and the snow, for to all seasons there is a purpose—just as *you* are always the purpose of the journey. You. You. You.

# CHAPTER TWENTY-SIX

# FORGIVENESS AND YOUR UNLIMITED POTENTIAL

Let us speak now of forgiveness. Forgiveness is never given to one who is undeserving...and you are *all* deserving. There is not one person, one incident, one thought, one moment that is not forgivable. To forgive is to show strength of purpose. To forgive is to take a step out of victimization and remove yet another veil of limit. To forgive is to become stronger in the process. When you are able to forgive a perceived wrong, you are ready to move beyond it. When forgiveness is not possible, you remain forever in its debt and continue to live in the state of checks and balances. You give to me, I give to you. You take, I give. I take, you give. Always there is a balance. It is believed that one should never take and take and take, or give and give and give. Where is the balance then?

Must you rate everything as to the level of its importance before forgiveness can be granted? No, for that is not the way of a truly forgiving heart. Why do I speak of the heart when I speak of forgiveness? Housed within that energy center is your love and connection to the All. The heart chakra is the core of all loving creation. But how do you forgive when your heart is broken? How do you put aside the hurt and begin to love again? How do you look upon any event in your life and forgive the injustice, pain or atrocities suffered? From this unrelenting emotion of remembered pain, the heart cries out and forgiveness seems impossible. To say you forgive when the heart is not in alignment is a false declaration and will never bring you the peace you seek.

When you dwell upon the cause of your pain and relive, analyze and compartmentalize the related emotions, you give it life, and forgiveness is not possible. You are only able to forgive when the feeling of ownership of any painful experience is no longer alive within you with the same intensity as before. At that moment, forgiveness is achieved, the veil is lifted and you are no longer a victim of any circumstance. You feel free, and it is indeed an exhilarating experience. One may think that to forgive a wrong means to let the perpetrators—the actors in the play of your forgiveness scenario—go without retribution of any kind. Releasing the feeling of being wronged with no further emotional attachment to the event means there would actually be an end to suffering. Sometimes the need to suffer takes on a life of its own and feeds a sense of righteousness. There are always at least two sides to any scenario of forgiveness, and one should be willing to look at all sides before declaring the veil truly lifted. Forgiveness comes before a lightened heart. The emotional release is immense and felt in an instant.

At one time or another, everyone on your planet has the opportunity to forgive and to be forgiven. When these events are viewed with an open mind and an open heart, they allow forgiveness to come in an instant of recognition. To truly forgive becomes an act of a seeking mind to move forward and evolve. When it is impossible to forgive and you are not willing to seek the deeper answer to your pain, look at this as simply another opportunity to evolve your human self. One must be willing to look upon his actions and reactions not for punishment but for the sake of forgiveness. First, forgive yourself, and then embrace what has brought the pain. When you view a painful experience from the place of victimization, you are not seeing through the eyes of the Self.

Look upon your reflection in the mirror of creation. You will not find yourself wanting. Quite the opposite. You will see a radiant being that is alive and free. My intention is not to cause more pain or judgment but to promote the realization that you are all the reflection of the Divine Spirit-Soul. When you can understand this, forgiveness won't exist in your reality—only allowance and perpetual movement forward. Scenarios of victimization are built around the limits of the mind and not from the place of who you are in truth. When you are ready to experience only from the Spirit-Soul perspective, forgiveness will never be an issue and you will be in continuous forward motion. What is behind you is forgotten and lifted from your consciousness. It is a process that you are learning as you journey and a choice you must make—to live in limit, or to move forward.

Take a breath and feel the difference in the air around you. Breathe in the shift in your conscious awareness as you make the leap outside limit. The air feels different here…lighter. It has a melody, a rhythm and a vibrational pulse all its own and helps to determine how your day will progress. There is an inherent synchronicity to your movements when you commit to live outside limits. You see your spark reflected in all things. Living outside limits for even a second of your time can bring you peace without equal. Even in the middle of a crowded room you will feel the surrounding peace. Walk more from within this realization and forgiveness will happen instantly because you have changed your view of life. You will live free and journey the path of true light. Each day you live is another opportunity to forgive and expand the Self. Once that is done, what causes you discomfort will never be of importance again.

When you stand on the threshold of new wisdom and begin to integrate its meaning, you will no longer look at your world as before. Through this door you find a world that is familiar, yet at the same time ever-changing and expanding. There is an ebb and flow to this new wisdom. Yet, surrounded by such change, you may be reluctant to surrender old beliefs. But this is about to change.

As you expand your view of heaven and earth and ponder old belief systems, take the time to view your life from a greater perspective and begin the process of "experiential propensity." This is an interesting word, is it not? *Propensity*: a tendency toward, or an inclination for something. I think it describes your position at this time quite well. You have a *propensity* for freedom. You have a *propensity* for truth and a *propensity* for peace. All these things can and are being achieved by you every day. You walk among your brethren while observing behaviors in yourself and others, continually seeking the knowledge of truth with an open mind and an open heart. This is a good place to be at this time. Now, having crossed the threshold of this portal called "the seeking mind," what awaits you there? When you are asked to look at the spaces in between the knowledge that is given, you must look in truth at how you live your life. It calls for accurate assessment and action. The spaces in between any wisdom and any truth are found through *action*. And you may apply this action through *observation*.

Let me give you an example. When you are told you are unlimited and can create what you wish once you're outside the box of limitations, do you accept this as truth even though you may have tried and failed on many occasions? Do you remember when I said that full expression of your creative force was not possible from within limits? If you remembered and forgave yourself for what you previously viewed as failure, then you were acknowledging the spaces in between and viewing the truth of your present reality. When I asked you to be the observer of your life and you were able to do so truthfully, then you were looking at the spaces in between. These were some of your greatest opportunities to move beyond limit.

When you observe your life through a limited point of view, creative force is vulnerable to a belief only in what is visible and tangible. What cannot be explained rationally is not accepted as truth. It is not easy to look between the lines to the deeper context when operating from limit and the human invents ways to engage the mind to keep from examining what lies between these lines. Within this limited perspective, the human entity has a tendency to become quite jaded. When babies are born, they have the ability to see between these lines quite easily. But this ability soon dims as a result of the limits imposed as they grow and develop. At this time in your transformational process, as the observer, you have the opportunity to expand your vision to see once more what others cannot.

What is your experience when you meditate? Is your mind infused with meaningless chatter? While in this meditative state, take note of where your attention is focused and the limits you are allowing. When your mind is open to accepting new possibilities and truths, old habits and beliefs slough away and new insights are integrated into a more expanded view. Embrace your evolving human self and use these experiences to journey realms yet to be explored. You are the observer and the participant in a constant state of change. Begin to live your life today outside the box. See the difference and begin to find your joy in transformation.

When you are discussing limits of any kind, always observe your personal behavior. This behavior is your life pattern. How you dress, your interests, facial expressions, body language and the way in which you react to life in general are all part of your life pattern. How you react and what you do when there is stress or pain in your life is indicative of your current beliefs. While these limits may define how you are viewed by the outside world, they are truly not all that you are. When you step outside the limited view, the truth begins to emerge.

If you are discontent with any situation in your life, step outside limited thought patterns and create a result more to your liking. When you do so for even a moment in your timing, peace can prevail. What changes? Does the situation or person suddenly become calm and submissive? Do the seas part, the sun break through or the rains stop? Do you hear trumpets heralding a new outcome? Perhaps it could happen this way if you wish. Anything is possible when you first commit to live without limit. More than likely, the only thing that will change is you and your peaceful surrender. Does that mean you will sit in a state of bliss with a smile on your face? No, although that might not be a bad start. What it means is that you silently said to the conscious mind, *I think I will consider another way of being.* And by just this one thought, you allowed yourself to release limit. You may feel this glimmer of peace for only a brief moment in time, but it is a beginning. Be willing to try. Some beliefs die hard. Giving up these strongly- held beliefs may cause you to fear losing the only Self that you know. You can never lose the Self, your identity, your spark from Original Thought. How could that even be possible? This is who you are and will be forever. I am simply asking you to release the limits that have kept you going around in circles, bumping into the walls of your own making and repeating patterns that prevent you from finding peace. This peace is synonymous with unlimited thought and is the direct result of your surrender to truth. When one feels free to explore, is unafraid to envision and willing to operate out of True Mind, peace is always the result.

So, in this future scenario, you take the leap and step outside limit for a brief moment while in the midst of a stressful situation. You remember that *peace is a result of unlimited thought.* You take a deep breath, physically step back and shift your focus for just a moment...and everything changes. You have just come forth into your unlimited potential. A sense of peace brought about through unlimited thought can be applied to many different scenarios. As you begin living your unlimited potential more often, the possibilities become endless.

Relax and enjoy the events of your life as they unfold throughout your day. Be patient. It is a good virtue to have, though it, too, has limits. When you are cautioned to be patient, you are being given a limit. I encourage you to become aware of limited thinking and, thus, are presenting an opportunity for you to question what you hear. Always question. Humans often avoid questioning information when they feel it is given by someone more knowledgeable. That is why you are so easily manipulated. "Blind faith" is a nice concept but wholly unsuited for our purpose. I want you to question. I want you to think outside the box of limitation and dogma and see clearly what lies before you on your journey. Your adventure is not for me to determine. I am giving you probabilities and insights that have been gained from my adventures. I am giving you my truths. You may accept them until you begin to expand and discover your own. That is the process of unlimited thought. Exploration. Speculation. Integration. Creation. It is a wonderful process indeed.

It is time for you to come forth into the act of being and believe in the Self. When you believe in the Self, you are able to live more and more outside the confines of limit. Take the opportunity to approach one stressful situation with peace uppermost in your mind and see what happens. The change may be subtle, or it may come upon you in a rush of insight and joy. If you pay attention to what is happening, you will be changed from that time forward. Hold the thought of peace in your conscious mind and repeat this phrase silently: *I am at peace.* It will assist you to remember. Let go of your need to remain burdened by limitation. Try a new way of being, for you are on an adventure. Always turn your focus forward, for what is behind you is gone forever. *What lies outside any pattern of limited thought is who you really are.* You are free to choose in any moment. Do not be discouraged if you are unable to accomplish this sense of peace instantly. Keep searching and focusing the thought process on peace. Be persistent and enjoy the quiet surrender that comes from living without limit.

Perhaps it is not enough to venture more outside limit without first observing what has been created from within the dichotomy of limited and unlimited existence. Be the observer, not in judgment but in acceptance, and gain a better understanding and appreciation for the wonders that have been created. When you can accept limit and begin to integrate it into your essence, the walls will come tumbling down. I have cautioned you to step outside the box of limitations when what I was truly asking and moving you toward was a unification of these limits within your unlimited being. When you can observe from this state of Oneness, you will truly be seeing and experiencing life.

When I speak of human life, know that it is spoken of with great reverence for the etheric, as well as the dense body mass that is you. Observe today. Absorb limit into your observation and integrate it within your unlimited being. Do this with a light heart and listen to the message between the lines. When limited and unlimited existences are truly lived as one with no separation, you will simply Be a complete and whole Being. It is toward this integration that we are headed. It is time to contemplate and integrate your life in limit, and, in the process, become unlimited thought projection. I challenge you to do this for even a portion of your day. You have your assignment. Now go forth and be happy that you are here at this timing. That you are here at all is the point.

# CHAPTER TWENTY-SEVEN

# THE SELF ON A JOURNEY OF DISCOVERY

Speak these words upon arising: "I welcome the dawning of this new day" and you will find that what has gone on before this moment in time has served the purpose of bringing you here. I do not speak of myself as a savior. Far from it. I am simply a guidepost along your path. You arrived at this time in your life not by chance but by a grand design brought about through community effort. This "community" numbers in the thousands, all focused on accomplishing a single goal: the complete realization of the Self as the spark from Original Thought. You are the Self in absolute forward motion with many wonderful opportunities yet to explore.

The Self on a journey of discovery is a sight to behold, with many starts and stops along the way. What do I seek to know? This is a question you must ask yourself at every opportunity. What do you, the Self personified, seek to know? Do you wish to know what is ahead of you? Do you want to fully understand what you've already experienced? Do you ask questions of your Spirit–Soul in meditation or prayer when you are free from distraction? If you do not, perhaps it is time that you did. But when you ask a question, you must be prepared to receive the answer. You may not like or always understand the answers, but you will learn from them just the same. You may ask the reason for an accident, illness or perceived failure and what can be learned from each experience. The possible questions from a seeker are endless. The need to examine in minute detail every aspect of your life is not necessary, for you are truly born anew in each moment. That is how your journey is able to continue through the muck and mire of gravity's pull and why I always encourage you to keep moving.

The Self continually changes and sparks with eternal life force. It never sleeps or rests. As the Self inhabiting human form, you are that spark of life force. You are continually moving and changing, growing and releasing and forever spiraling outward in your search to realize the truth of your existence. There is no turning back. What has gone on before the time you've spent reading this, is gone forever. When you speak "I think I will rest a bit right here and right now," do so if you must, but you truly can never stop and rest on life's journey. If that is your belief, then when you die you'll begin the sleep of the unaware Spirit-Soul. These are the human sparks that would wait and rest until Jesus came to wake them up, when the world was ready for resurrection through Him. These entities would slumber until they decide to awaken and embrace their true potential as blessed sparks from the Source. Only then would their spirit guides have the opportunity to assist them forward on their journey.

If you are one who would journey with eyes wide open, mind fully engaged and a Spirit that seeks the truth, it is to you I speak. Come join me in an all-encompassing meditative state. Perhaps you believe a meditative state can only be reached while sitting in a lotus position, with hands resting on the knees and eyes focused inward on the third eye. It may be what some of you were taught, but this is really only another kind of dogma. *The meditative state can be accomplished by simply living the truth that you seek.* By stating what you want each dawn, being grateful and aligning yourself with the joy and happiness of seeking truth, you are in a perpetual state of meditation. Some of you may question the validity of this statement and choose to follow the beliefs you find difficult to give up. If you think the religious conservatives of your day are the only dogmatic individuals on this planet, you will be surprised to discover that arrogance lives in all of you. This arrogance inhibits change and prevents growth. This is not a criticism but an opportunity to be aware of the prevalence of certain dogmatic beliefs that exist in all of humankind. Continue to practice your quiet, peaceful meditations in solitude when you wish, but also acknowledge and experience fully those meditative moments that occur throughout your day as seekers of the wisdom of the Spirit-Soul— the Self personified.

The human, earthbound life is measured in moments of time. There is a beginning, middle and an end that is predictable and which follows a pattern of birth to death with all of the stages in between. As you have embraced human form to live your journey this time around, nothing appears to alter that cycle. I wish to share certain insights that can provide the opportunity to experience a more enlightened life expression. Will only a privileged few achieve enlightenment? No. This information and encouragement for further exploration of the Self is given freely to everyone and with great joy. I will not tell you how to live your life. My purpose is to give you as much information and insight as possible so you make choices that bring you peace in the knowledge of who you are. I have watched your human evolution on planet earth and observed many similar planets throughout the many galaxies. I find your planet to be one of the most intriguing. I am drawn here because many of you are on an evolutionary cusp, from limited human expression to full realization of the Self. Will your human body cease to exist when this happens? No. You will simply expand your knowledge of the Self and continue to journey from a more enlightened perspective. How this will be expressed will be as individual as the humans inhabiting this planet.

A number of enlightened individuals on your planet have authored books or become spiritual teachers to the masses. But there are also those who live quietly in remote villages, in towns and cities, and don't write books or lecture. They do not attend spiritual gatherings, and you may never know of their existence unless you chance to meet them. They are the ones who make a place in their heart for you and can lift your spirit with a smile or encouraging word. It may be someone who gives you a hand with a heavy package or opens the door when you are in a hurry and lets you pass ahead of them. These enlightened beings wear many faces and would not deem themselves greater than you at all. Yet they have achieved a sense of quiet peacefulness that is like a magnet to those who are searching. Pay attention to the people you encounter. Practice your peaceful smile and become more Self-aware as you journey. With these small steps you gain the highest reward.

Each kindness that is given holds an energy that echoes around the world. In the process, everything and everyone is changed and elevated in the Light. Resolve to live this way and your momentum toward enlightenment will be inevitable. Evolution is never stagnant; it's always alive with movement and energy. Find opportunities to promote kindness in your world. Take a step back from judgment and breathe in the air of forgiveness and eternal peace. If you do so honestly, you will find peace, kindness and forgiveness returned to you in abundance. I won't be the one to wave a magic wand and speak "You are enlightened." You are the one who will do the work; I simply provide a course of study and contemplation. You bring forth what you already know in truth. That is why I am here—to wake you up to that realization. I would not be here if I didn't think you were capable.

As you begin to practice acts of kindness and forgiveness, you may be surprised to find how little you forgive yourself. I say forgive it *all*— the past, the present and anything you judge negatively. If you live in a perpetual state of peaceful surrender and kindness, what is there to forgive? Do not look behind you, for you have moved beyond the past. First, be kind to yourself and find your peace. Then let this beauty flow from you. Your rewards will increase ten-fold. Pay attention to your life, and smooth those corners where the edges seem too sharp. Do so in the name of your evolution. You don't have to sell the house, auction off all your possessions or leave your family and friends. You may choose, instead, to expand Self-awareness from within your present life expression, and all will change as you change. When I ask you to be the observer, it is to have you continually mindful of what is occurring in your life. Will every day be without stress of any kind? Probably not. The process of growth can often seem stressful. It would be wise to let go of those occasions that disrupt your peace as soon as they no longer serve a purpose. (And they do have a purpose, or you wouldn't have created them). You are the one who must decide whether or not to punish yourself with regret. Be the observer of your thoughts and beliefs—it will help you to know where you are in the continuum of the evolving Spirit-Soul. Be in peace. And remember to come forth into the act of being and believe in the Self. If you have come this far, it is the way you have chosen it to be.

Many spiritual Masters, past and present, have shared a simple truth: the life you are living now as a human is, in reality, a dream of your own creation. And though this is indeed true, it is often difficult to comprehend a dream while living in it. What you have always believed to be your waking state is really an illusion created for emotional experience. Some of you understand that quite well. Whether or not you believe you were created by God, Original Thought or from a little sperm and egg, you know you exist because, well, here you are! You are experiencing your journey in a human life form and are the creator of that form and the events surrounding it. You may ask, "If this is my dream, why would I choose to suffer? Why am I not living in a manor house with abundant wealth? Why am I sick, and my pocket book empty? Why am I alone?" If your current life isn't a happy one, you might create a future lifetime where you build that mansion, experience love and have the money, beauty and fame you deem important to your wellbeing. On this wheel of reincarnation, you created a new life, died that lifetime, came back to live once again, died, came back, ad infinitum—in and out of this dream called human life. Mankind, you have been dreaming for a very long time. This is a planet of dreamers. But it is also a planet where some of you are awakening and creating life from a different perspective altogether. I have watched you awaken from your dream, take a step out of limit and embrace the truth that has existed from the beginning. In the beginning, Original Thought/God looked out across the heavens and spoke that this was good and the universal order would be populated with peaceful, loving sparks who would, in turn, create on into forever. I speak to you of things that have always been. I speak to you of things that exist now and those that are coming. Waking from the slumber of limitation and illusion can be difficult, yet always rewarding. Some of you will be content to live repeatedly in your created dream, while others will explore new realms. Make the choice that serves you best.

When first you awaken from your nightly slumber, do you get up groggy and fumble about? Does it take you time to come fully awake, or do you bound out of bed refreshed and eager for your day? Do you remember portions of your sleep-filled dream? You have such a variety of wonderful experiences in human slumber, it is a wonder any of you wake at all! When the human body is laid to rest for the night or takes a nap and closes off the human conscious mind for even a short period of time, the Spirit-Soul is transported to a wholeness embraced in truth. From this place you are once more given the opportunity to adventure as a universal consciousness without the veils of forgetfulness. It is a wonderfully productive time, and you are often reluctant to come back to your created dream here on earth. Alarm clocks of all shapes and sizes have been created to bring you back to this illusion. During human slumber, with eyes closed, breath slowed, muscles relaxed and the mind free of distraction, you return to the True Self. What is experienced in the sleep state is similar to what can be found during the practice of meditation. This illusion you have created called "being human" is really just a little side trip to your true existence. Some no longer feel the need to experience life on your planet and seek new adventures on their path to Self-exploration. Some will choose to remain in this dream. It is not judged either way; it is simply your choice.

For those of you who seek new pathways to truth, taking steps outside limit is a beginning. Reading missives such as these, making contact with like-minded people, exploring new options and opening the mind through meditation will help you find answers. You are on an adventure where it may be timely for you to ask this question: "Do I continue on as before, or grab the brass ring being offered?"—metaphorically speaking, that is. Pay attention to everything and, as the constant observer of your life, you will gain greater and greater insight. Try it. This is knowledge you can put to use right away. When you separate the truth from the dream you call your life, you become an evolutionary human that will journey and expand each unique experience. How this is accomplished will be up to you.

I speak to you as one among many sparks from the Source who have willingly explored new possibilities, seen what few have seen and experienced what few have dared. As we journeyed uncharted territory, we shared these experiences with others of like mind. The fact that we came to inhabit your planet during its formative stage was unusual to some of our compatriots. We were here to not only experience and record the nature of planetary formation but also to study the outcome of specific behaviors on our fellow explorers. The experience gained was invaluable, and we were able to learn a great deal regarding human consciousness. You might say we were the first pioneers of behavioral science. We came with a sense of adventure and relatively few expectations. Some of the original inhabitants still return to check on your development from time to time and help those who wish to further their evolution.

Can this planet be saved from further destruction? That is entirely up to you, its inhabitants. In true fact, there have always been two planets co-existing from the beginning of your earth. One resides in a dimensional awareness that is akin to elevated consciousness, and one resides in this dimensional existence that remains tenuous at best. The one you are presently experiencing has been on the brink of destruction for several years, as evidenced by the melting of the polar icecaps, the depleted ozone layer, the devastating weather patterns and the burgeoning population. The disrespect for all life and this planet as a whole is a dangerous path to follow. I would tell you this: the earth's population resides in both expressions but with very different outcomes, which are dependent upon the treatment of your planet and the welfare of its inhabitants. We are attempting to elevate this destructive-prone planet to merge completely with the more expansive one. An interesting theory, is it not? There are those who would say that there cannot possibly be two dimensional levels to earth's existence. I would say why not? Actually, there are many more than two levels. Some of you have such limited beliefs that even imagining the idea of multiple realities may be difficult to grasp. There are not only many dimensional levels to earth's existence but multiple levels of human experience as well. You have the ability to simultaneously experience different probable outcomes to any experience. Perhaps you wish to change an event where you have lost a loved one and then go back in time and prevent this from occurring. That is understandable, but it also brings change in many more lives than your own. The ripple effect of such a change in outcome in one dimension could be felt throughout the world and even throughout the universal order. But still some of you will attempt it.

There is a way to safely experience a different outcome to an event without having an effect on anyone but yourself—that is by using the dream state you call slumber. Will the experience seem real? Yes, as real as any that you are experiencing now. When you wake, will you remember? Maybe not. But what you will have are moments of conscious insight. Back from slumber, you might find yourself contemplating, *If my daughter had lived, she would be married now, or in college,* and you would find peace instead of pain. When this occurs, you might reflect on the reason for that peace. More than likely, you were witness to this very scenario, lived it, gained wisdom and released the pain of separation—all in a moment's slumber. This altered scenario causes no ripples through time or in the fabric of the universal order. It was created for you, by you, to find peace through the attainment of higher wisdom. This occurs often without your conscious knowledge, for you are multi-layered beings with the ability to experience many events simultaneously. Your existence is truly a tapestry that has many threads woven together with great care and insight. Take these insights and make them your own, even when they seem beyond belief. But do so in your own timing.

*This latest insight from Mother brought to mind a dream I had one night. In this dream, I saw myself with a little girl around age six. She was my daughter and we were walking to town to see her father, my husband. This was a wonderful dream and healed a wound I had carried for many, many years from the loss of my own daughter at birth. I woke in such joy and felt the grief from her absence finally lifted from my heart. In this dream, this other reality, we were together and living our life in happiness. I feel blessed to have had this opportunity to experience the truth of what Mother shared about our being multi-layered beings.*

You are in a play of your own choosing, and you have chosen to receive this information at just this time. The wheels are turning in the minds of those committed to come forth into the act of being, and I ask you to believe in the Self as never before. You are unlimited beings, where everything is possible. Don't become lost trying to change the past into a better outcome. There is no better outcome; it is simply what you have created in order to learn. Changing the outcome of any experience doesn't make life better; it simply makes it different. Trust your initial experience as the one that was created by you for the opportunity to learn and journey higher wisdom. Going back to undo a supposed wrong is never recommended. It is why I encourage you to continually move forward. Don't linger in the "what-ifs" of the past. As the creator of your life adventure, you will have many experiences. Learn from them, and always keep moving forward.

# CHAPTER TWENTY-EIGHT

# I AM AWAKE

The Self is the universal connection to your origin. The Self is the vehicle that transports you from limit to all possibility and truth, and will reveal the true purpose of your being. Complete awareness of the Self is an ongoing process. Jesus experienced similar moments of awareness and growth during His lifetime, though not from the particularly limited perspective that you have today. He remains a wonderful example of what is currently happening for many of you. Though it is often difficult to separate the man from the myth, Jesus' lifetime holds great meaning and promise for all who are on this journey of awakening. He accomplished what you are attempting, breathed life into the Self and became, for many, the living example of what can be accomplished when trust and connection to the truth is complete. Jesus transcended this earthly life to expand beyond the Self contained in human form, and continued his journey on the way to new adventures. Can you do anything less? Throughout your history, there have been those who have followed Jesus' example. No written records or great stories of their birth or lifetime have been written; but nonetheless, they transcended their earthly existence and moved forward to embrace the Self in total awareness. The recognition and acceptance of the Self as the spark from Original Thought—the vehicle for your human life and further adventure—is an important part of your evolution. You don't have to go into the desert for forty days and nights before revelations and messages from the Self can be known to you. Don't get caught up in the fictional story of Jesus. He was who you are. What His journey was in truth was not always written of accurately. There was a man called Jesus, and He walked the path you are walking. He lived within limits, just as you do and left these limits behind when He transcended as the Self and became a traveler through time once more. You can and will do no less, for you have willed it so. Jesus is ever your companion and your mirror to gaze upon. He broke ground for this adventure of the realized Self and cleared the path of obstacles that were His to overcome. He loves you that much, and even more. You would do well to model your behavior after what He has accomplished. He showed you the way. The way was not pain and suffering—that was merely to gain your attention—but instead was filled with beauty and revelation. You can do nothing less.

The Self is your connection to Original Thought and, as such, has never changed in truth or purpose. Within this realization has come the free will to express upon the path as you choose. The question now becomes how to listen once more to the Self while living within the limits of the human existence. How can one find the truth? The answer is a simple one: *listen to the Self.* In times of meditation and quiet contemplation, you can make a connection through the unconscious mind. To connect consciously, be the observer and receive guidance from the Self to gain wisdom. The combination of these disciplines of meditation, contemplation and observation will be a powerful force from which to access the Self. I leave it up to you.

In the event that you find yourself unable to access the Self and are still wondering how you would know if you did anyway, I will lay out a few guideposts. When you rise in the morning, speak these words: "I am awake." This might seem obvious, but within this statement is another meaning altogether. To be truly awake is to be conscious of what is occurring in your life. When you speak "I am awake," you are committing yourself to journey in a truth-finding adventure for that day. It is a simple declaration intended to start your engines, so to speak. Go about your daily chores and smile more often at the world around you. If you listen to the news or read the paper, you may not see much to smile about. I am asking you to release the limits that surround and distract you, and to observe at a deeper level. The news media reporting the death and destruction and follies of mankind is only there to divert you, and unnecessary for your purpose. This is not the intent of the phrase *I am awake.*

As you go about your day, speak "I am awake" more often. Speak it in your mind. *I am awake.* Then observe the result. Should you expect a lightening bolt of awareness to strike between your feet? Well, that would open your eyes for sure, but perhaps a gentler awakening would be better. The insights gained from these daily observations are very important. If you fail to assimilate knowledge from these experiences, you may need to repeat them more times than you might wish. Perhaps that is why one sees history often repeated—because of man's failure to realize and integrate the truth more fully while living it.

*I realized, after listening to this message from Mother, the times in my life I had remained in a situation when it didn't bring me happiness, or succumbed to the negativity around me. Saying "I am awake" is for me, the opposite of continuing to poke your eye with a stick when you know it will never bring you the peace you seek. I use this phrase often, as the observer, to keep to my path of self-knowledge and truth, and it truly does bring me peace.*

When you state, "I am awake," you are working on your awareness of the Self within any given scenario. Be honest in the evaluation of what you discover when you use this simple phrase, *I am awake,* until you slumber once more. Allow the dream state of awareness to carry you through the journey into other realms that will hasten your awakening even more. It is a beginning. Always, it is a beginning. It can be nothing else and serve you. The rhythm and synchronicity that flow between what is seen as spirit realm and what is determined to be human expression will be complete when you rise and speak "I am awake." It is the beginning, the middle and the end that can never be. To be awake is the goal. *I am awake* carries with it the energy vibration of Original Thought, God-essence. When spoken upon arising, it begins the day with renewed connection and hope. When spoken in the mind throughout the day, it provides the energy and motivation to continue on in awareness.

There are so many opportunities to fully awaken yet at the same time, many roadblocks that seem to interfere. Still, you rise to face a new day and you continue. This grand intention to continue is something to honor with utmost care. When one speaks "I am awake," it also carries with it the intention "and I shall continue," which is then spoken together as one statement: "I am awake and I shall continue." When these two phrases are repeated and integrated within the mind of the Spirit-Soul, all possibility is realized. How one expresses these thoughts throughout his day is a reflection of the power and extent of his integrative process. Can you do anything less then attempt this integration of Spirit-Soul and human expression? I think not. My scribe and I are communing in perhaps a most unusual way. I say "perhaps unusual" because this means of scribing wisdom has existed since the beginning of life force on your planet and will continue until the last days. Do not fret when I speak of the last days. I only mean a time when there is no longer a need to read words on a page and you can access information on your own, for there will be no separation. Some have envied her ability to listen and transcribe words on a page and the connection we share. They don't understand that they, too, are spoken to all the time but neglect to use their ability to truly listen. She listens and hears me not with the ears of human expression but with the yearning of her Spirit-Soul to connect with the Self of her Being and to be as One in unison of purpose. Our process is somewhat unique but not without difficulty. When we connect as One, her process of letting go of limitation is most important so that the layers of resistance can be peeled away. The difference between the flow of information when she is resistant and when she is at One with the message is very clear to her, as it should be. I speak to you of things that will evolve your soul, not of things that will entertain or bring acceptance from those who may read these missives. We are not about convincing or cajoling anyone to follow where we lead. We present what will be needed for your transformation, and move on.

Do not become lost in the wars and fighting of the present time upon the earth. All this hatred will soon burn down and melt like candle wax upon the earth. The cleansing of this dark vibrational energy is coming to an end and the dark forces will be destroyed from within. The human is quite unique in its capacity to embrace opportunities to expand, while at the same time creating limitations that interfere with Self journey. As you become aware of these created distractions, they will cease to exist. Join together with those of like mind and send the thoughts of peace and joy out into the swirling universal energy that encircles your planet. Tap into this powerful flow of joyful peace when you forget to remember.

When you have an illness of the body, do you get well by focusing on the illness or on the state of health? It is the same with any desired outcome. When you focus on the war and destruction and not on the joy of peace, you are unable to create the desired effect. I say to you now: *take the time to create joyful peace in your world.* Concentrate the energy of your Spirit-Soul and your human mind toward this outcome, and so it shall be. Great wisdom has been accomplished and integrated within the cells of the body just by taking this one single step. Contemplate what you bring to this planet by your presence here. It is not a simple task I ask of you. It may take some time for you to determine how you want to achieve the simple outcome of the statement, *I am awake and I shall continue.* I introduce this now so you'll understand that we have traversed great distances from just this simple contemplation. I am not one who has come to give you a roadmap, though I will leave you guideposts along the way. I will not give you steps to follow, numbering them as I go. No. You, who are reading and integrating these missives, have walked these roads before. You are adventurers searching for another layer of meaning to your life and seeking your transformational spirit through contemplation, observation and integration. I would see you be joyful in the process. And why would you choose to be anything else? As you recognize and operate from the truth of the Self as you understand it to be, you have the opportunity to live and interact in the world from a more expanded view. Will you be a happier individual? Yes, indeed, for it is a natural consequence when one expands beyond the physical. Will you neglect home, family, work, friends and civic duties? No, of course not. But if this is the excuse you give for delaying your forward momentum, then view it as such honestly.

How will you know when you are living and operating more from within the Self than the human? Full integration of the Self is like a dance, synchronized and moving in such a way that your life becomes lighter, happier and more in tune with the world around you. When you experience a misstep or tread on some toes but survive anyway, well, that is more the human expression. Can the Self and the human merge as One? Most definitely. And this is the path you have chosen to walk this time around. Did you think the body must die and you must experience what is called "soul deliverance" in order to come together with the Self completely? No. And it is not why you have come to read these missives, or why my scribe sits with me in the morning to record, contemplate and observe. When you can illume the body and dance the dance of the Self in tandem with human existence, you are ready to accelerate the process of Oneness. This is the opportunity presented to you at this time.

The world around you may seem too chaotic to ever change, as wars continue to rage, crimes are committed and disease is prevalent. But at the same time, for every negative there is a positive. It is as it has always been and will always be in a world that is for the purpose of exploration and evolution. The chaos that surrounds you is similar to white noise and an attempt to divert your attention from truth. *It is successful only if you choose to focus your attention there.* Yes, there are people dying and the environment is suffering. And yes, there are valid issues to be addressed which have been created through human cooperation and agreement. But for some time now, your world has been experiencing an evolution of spirit consciousness that is rapidly gaining attention and acceptance within the general population and even in the mass media. More often than not, when these shifts of consciousness occur, there is increased upheaval in the world. It is historically accurate. In times of peace and prosperity, there is little drive toward the esoteric. Comfort is found in the ritual of church dogma, in the family and in the predictability of life. Not everyone in this scenario is without strife. Some may even begin to question their present reality, but for the most part, these few share a quiet revolution.

When the search for truth becomes the new mantra and the determination to connect to the Self takes on new life, oftentimes the serious nature of outside distractions escalates. How do you overcome these distractions and continue to evolve? Speak, "I am awake and I will continue" and set your feet solidly upon your path, and the roadblocks will begin to fall away. Make your focus the Self-realized journey, not life's distractions. Can you separate yourself completely from what is occurring in the world? No. But you can care, support those in need, maintain your human responsibilities and still remain focused on the journey of the Self. You have the opportunity to integrate the spiritual within the human expression and make the Self the central theme to your day—every day. When distractions occur, ask yourself how it furthers your evolution to give them your attention. What do you gain if you focus on the melting polar icecaps or on the wars and poverty? To some it may seem a heartless viewpoint, centered entirely on selfish interest. They would be correct about where your focus is centered. You are about the evolution of the Self, and no roadblocks, outside opinion or circumstance will distract you from this path. Do you understand as yet that these outside distractions are man-made? They are manifested exclusively from the agreement between certain individual and group souls who are on a different journey than yours. It should not be allowed to interfere with your goal of the realized Self, as it is *their* journey. It is good for you to know that someone does not die in a war because you were not totally focused on that one distraction to the Self. You do not have the ability to determine how another will experience life or death. You must begin to understand that the distractions or roadblocks along your path to the Self will always be there in one form or another. Where you place your intent and focus will determine whether these distractions keep you from moving forward or are simply registered as mere blips on your life screen. Life happens. These distractions have nothing to do with your journey, unless you decide they do. You have not come to this place in time privy to this information because you were out of balance; quite the contrary. Acknowledge your existence as it is today. Change what does not serve you, and go on from there. You are not selfish or self-serving when you are on this journey of the Self. It is during this time that you are more loving and giving and wholly present in the Light for the betterment of all mankind. As such, you can influence all who come within your sphere, whether it is the person in front of you in line at the marketplace or your family and friends as a whole. Remember this: *as you change, all around you begins to change.*

Do you find your life chaotic or peaceful? Be honest in your answer. Where there is chaos, a roadblock exists to be removed and wisdom to be gained in the process. When there is peace, you have another job to do—focus and seek your purpose. Do not blindly go about your day in a state of Samadhi—in peaceful oblivion to the outside world—for it will not serve your purpose. You must keep your mind engaged and active. Seek wisdom from within the realm of your human existence. Remember that your purpose is the merging of the two—the human and the Self—into the One who is fully committed to the journey of evolution. What did Jesus do? He prayed when it was time to pray, experienced life as a human when it was time to live in the body, and eventually merged the human and the Self into the One and transcended earthly experience to continue. Can you do anything less? You may not have a story written about your life as He did, but you will have an effect on the world just the same simply because of the journey you have chosen to pursue at this time.

I have given you much to contemplate and would have you bless your families, the world you live in, the peacekeepers and the warmongers as well. The wars and strife will continue until the agreement for it among the masses dissipates and the path of cruelty toward one another is no more. It is happening with every step you take toward the Self and the balance to be found within the human body. You cannot solve a problem if you are not aware one exists. This has been an attempt to isolate a problem and present a solution. The problem is the agreements that lead to chaos and cruelty in your world, and the solution is to focus mankind to come forth and believe in the Self without question. Go about your day and integrate each distraction into focused Self-realization and see what occurs outside the parameters of your limited perspective. The power of focused prayer/ meditation is one way to influence change. Use it and you will see. I am forever continuing on my path. Are you?

*I am awake* carries with it the hope and the faith and the knowledge that has been buried deep within the molecular structure of your body. The ability to move through your daily life with an awakened spirit alive and sparking within you to come forth is the direction for your path at the moment. There may be detours and roadblocks along the way, but with each day you are beginning to move through doubt and fear and more into the realm of the adventure called "coming home." This is not a final destination, as is the second part of the mantra of awakening, *I will continue.* This means exactly what it says. The "home," of which I have often spoken, is the one of the enlightened Spirit-Soul. From there, your adventure continues in a new direction of all possibility and opens new vistas that have yet to be explored. There is no stopping place. The belief of those who would tell you that the final destination for humankind is heaven is limited at best.

You may find yourself standing at the precipice of all knowledge and truth, and yet you hesitate. Though the sense of adventure may keep some of you moving forward, there are many who wish to linger in what is familiar.

These humans live each day as complete and are not motivated to look beyond tomorrow. They have their own little area of expertise. They speak that they are good at their job, have a wonderful family and friends, and have love, good health and wellbeing. What more could there be? It is a good question and a perfect example of the limited thought process. Do not be fooled into thinking you are about the Self when you reason like this. You have chosen to stay within the box of limitation and have no desire to leave. When one is busy living his life, the balance of awareness is more in the physical and the concrete and everything that can be touched, seen, heard, felt and experienced in the physical is his reality. There is no room for esoteric contemplation, and meditation is just something the guru on the mountaintop and a few misguided New Age people practice. These humans are living in limit, and loving it. So where do they go from there? In most cases, they don't go anywhere except where they have always been. What is familiar brings them a sense of security. But those of you who desire change and continue to search will break free and experience beyond your physicality and limit. When you are willing, sit quietly, breathe deeply and surrender into a place of peace through the practice of meditation or prayer. It is there that the opportunity to connect to a deeper understanding of the intricacies of the Self and the origin of your birth is possible. Through such dedication and focus, the world is changed. An example of one such change can be found in the current mainstream acceptance of meditation, the practice of yoga, the search for balance in life and spirituality in general.

To access the Self as your guide, it is helpful to practice meditation. Find a quiet place where you can be undisturbed, get comfortable, then close your eyes and begin to breathe slowly and with focus. When you meditate and go within, you find the answer to questions directly from the Self. You have no better teacher. The Self is limitless and pure in composition. The Self teaches you the origin of your birth. The Self will speak to you of Original Thought and your lifetime now, and help you to consider each step wisely. The Self may speak words through another to guide you, or place you in situations to help you learn and grow in self-awareness. The Self will give you courage when needed and a sense of peace when desired. The Self is the central character in your play called life on planet earth. Give yourself the opportunity to access this wellspring of complete knowledge. Do not hesitate to call upon the Self and make it a daily practice.

# CHAPTER TWENTY-NINE

# CROSSROADS

It is time to increase your desire to become more the Self and less the human expression. Awaken in the morning and ignite the passion to remember and live truth as presented each day. Expand your mind to encompass all that has been given to you, and then you will know and live the Self as Original Thought personified. Gain wisdom and begin to apply it as truth. But perhaps this isn't what you wish to do at this time. You may be very comfortable living within the parameters set forth by you and society. It may seem relatively safe to remain just as you are. I would never tell you that you *should* want to expand the mind or that you *should* wish to explore other realms or that you *should* leave anything behind that you presently value—for then you would believe there is something wrong with you. There is nothing wrong with you. I cannot emphasize this enough.

I am here to bring you information and the knowledge of the beginning. I am here to awaken that knowledge in your very cells. I am here to see that you have all the information you need and then to support you in every way possible when you decide to act upon this information. I have always told you that you have free will. It is inherent in everything you do and have done since the inception of your birth into being. You have the ability to create what you want when viewing truth from outside limitation. This is actually a misconception, for, in fact, you create all the time, whether you do so from within your box of limitations or while functioning in an unlimited state of awareness. The creations are different, but they are still a result of your choice. Free will can be complicated, and it takes an illuminated mind and significant wisdom to give it the justice it deserves.

I am attempting to educate your mind—your True Mind—which encompasses both the conscious and the unconscious. I would like you to appreciate and respect your inherent wisdom, which touches everything you project into your life. It is up to you to decide what emotional baggage you carry with you and how you present yourself at any given moment, for you possess the wisdom to make informed choices. That is all. I would simply have you better armed to go out and greet your day.

How do you know when you have made choices from an illuminated perspective? Simply look around you. Is there peace in your life? Do you wake up in the morning with a smile on your face? Do you greet each apparent obstacle with a light heart? Do you marvel that you are here at all, experiencing every possible emotion and continually able to find peace and happiness in the process? More insights will come as you step outside limit and embrace and expand unlimited expression. Then you will know. There may still be occasions in your life that cause pain, and when I ask you to have the courage to step outside limits and embrace truth; I do not do so lightly. I understand there may be the pull of certain soul attachments not so easily relinquished. If that is the case, stay within these limits until you are ready to let them go. Gain what you will from any perceived roadblocks along the way. They're only temporary and will not hinder the path you travel.

Mankind, if you understand nothing else, understand this simple fact: you have accepted a journey of truth, transformation and illumination. And nothing, absolutely nothing, will keep you from the eventuality of this accomplishment. You are on a path that has many obstructions. Some may delay you. Others may cause pain or emotional challenges. But you will continue. You have the free will to move around, over or through any interference, when you so desire. I have simply come to encourage you to continue to move.

*In the course of recording these daily messages and tending to family, my job and other life events, it would sometimes become too overwhelming. It proved frustrating not to have the time or luxury to process everything that was being given. At those times—and there were several along the way—Mother would speak to me about*

*my journey. I share the following message on facing our "crossroads" as a testament
for all of us who journey this path:*

You have come to that fork in the road and may feel a division of energies,
a doubting of perception or even a questioning as to what it all means. This
is a good place to be, for it affords you the opportunity to reassess your life
and how you have lived it so far. It has come about from your searching
mind. It is good to pause and reassess before taking flight once more. It
is how an adventure evolves. There are many questions that have to be
asked and answered, and blind faith in certain outcomes is never necessary.
You may continue to have faith that what is being given to you is accurate
and for purposeful good. I will never tell you an untruth. I ask nothing
of you except that you listen, contemplate and adventure. But most of all,
I ask you to continue and give yourself permission to journey, and to ask
questions along the way. At times, you may even wish to take another path
altogether. So, when I say you may find yourself at yet another crossroads
and be questioning and experiencing doubt, anger or even disappointment,
this is to be expected. To be here at all is brilliant. Never forget that.

There are millions of your fellow humans who will never reach beyond
where they are standing—not for a very long time, anyway. In conscious
awareness of your journey, you have gathered around you people who
are also seeking. It is always so, that like are attracted to like and see the
spark within the souls of those they choose to be around. Would you
return to a state of ignorance and lethargy? Perhaps, but only when you
find yourself at such a crossroads or questioning point. It is good to ask
yourself this question: *Would I choose to go back if I could?* If the answer is
yes, then by all means attempt it. Go back to where you have been. Look
around you, even if you do so only in your mind or waking dream state.
Imagine what it will look like, the smell, the taste, the emotion, the very
atmosphere that you breathe. Seek what, for you, is in the past, and live
it once again. It is your dream, so make it what you will. Change the
scenario to suit your purpose and the outcome more to your liking. Do
it, and be truthful in your appraisal. Look around you at what you have
created in order to return. Are you the same? No. This is the one thing
that you can never deny. You may not be recognized in this recreation
of the past you attempt to create. What do I mean by this? I mean that
you have forever changed. You've moved on, adventured, grown and

changed. Your very perception has been altered. What is in the past is a different box of limits that did not include the new you. You cannot go backward through time, for when you continue to move as I have asked you to do, the past is altered forever. What is behind you leaves a vapor trail of experience. What is ahead of you, when seen through the eyes of one who knows how to vision, is endless and full of potential. You have already made the choice to continue on, or you would not find yourself at a crossroads. You have come to understand that I speak the truth as you begin to move through just such an experience.

A crossroads is an opportunity. What you seek will be an abundance of choice. You will know how to choose because that is what adventuring is all about—the freedom to experience what is before you. To wake each day and say, "I am ready" is a powerful statement. I can now bring you what I know of the journey, for you are at a crossroads and seek to *know* more than you wish to remain in limit. It is why I am here talking with you in such a manner. Mankind has become a master at walking through life as if in deep slumber, with occasional bouts of wakefulness and learning. I want to keep you awake more than you slumber. Take the time to rest when you need to, but ask yourself every day, *do I seek to slumber, or do I seek to be awake?* Some days it may be a toss-up, and that is alright, too. It is your journey. Perhaps you may choose to begin your day with the intention, *I am awake* and then see what transpires. The opportunities are vast, indeed.

I leave you with a choice, for I cannot teach you any more until you stop looking behind you. Until that time, I wait and continue to give you points to ponder. I have faith that you will continue. What you seek is before you. The knowledge that is past and worthy of remembrance is already imbued within the cells of your body. All other past experience is but a dream that can never be recaptured. It has served its purpose, or you would not be here at all. To stand at a crossroads is to acknowledge that you are continuing, have only paused in your journey for a bit and will be looking toward the coming light soon. It is the way of a seeking Spirit–Soul. I bid you a peaceful journey and wakefulness without end."

You may ask who I am, and I tell you that I am your whispered prayer for a better day, a song of the living and a signpost along the way to forever. I am what you are. It is as simple as that. When I say that we are One, I speak the truth. Who am I? Better to question why you would ask this of me now? I have called myself Mother at this time because that is how my scribe has known me in the past. Does it matter what other names I have been called throughout time? Do not get lost in the need to know, for who I am is unimportant in this process. And what is this process? This process is simply one of awakening and continuing to move forward. Once fully awake, you can do nothing else except continue. When you are in the process of awakening fully, you must be prodded a bit now and then to keep moving until the momentum gathers speed and becomes the only thing you want to do.

Who am I? I guess you could say I am your wakeup call. I come to this scribe because she will listen and make what I say available to others. I am not your master, your guru, your swami, your priest, your mother or your father. I am simply the one who has come to know and love the one who scribes my words and mankind as a whole. I have come to talk with you about what has been, what is and what will be. I have come to help you write the script for your participation in your journey, armed with as much knowledgeable truth as possible. It is not a simple task (mankind is not as receptive as it could be), but it is still a task worth doing. There are many who come with messages of peace and dedication to truth. Choose wisely. Don't listen to those who would manipulate the truth for personal gain. These messages are universal and for everyone, be they rich, poor, sane, insane, corrupt or honest. They are for *everyone*. I speak to the Self that is the central theme of any human expression. The Self is the vehicle, the Spirit-Soul, the spark from Original Thought. It is who you are, and you are brilliant!

When you journey, you take on different guises in order to adventure and to express life as a human. Yet the Self is always constant and will never change from the original intent. In this lifetime, those of you who read these missives are seeking to know and understand the Self. By doing so, you are attempting to strengthen the connection—long-denied—to the spark of Original Thought where it all began. I have taken you back to the beginning and given you many stories of your past. I have attempted to dispel certain myths and have introduced truth upon truth until you began to see with more than limited vision. I have encouraged you to look between the layers of present human existence and to move through these limits. Now you have come to another crossroads, where there are new choices to be made. Some choices involve balancing everyday life with more esoteric expansion. It becomes difficult to walk the line between the two as one or the other takes precedence. How can you fit your present human life into your search for completion? Perhaps you understand now why some monks live on mountaintops in monasteries, away from everyday distractions. In some ways it makes it easier to be totally devoted to journey and focused on one goal. This is not how the majority of you will do it. I say "will" do it because what I want you to know, without equivocation, is that you are in this process right now. My scribe has been walking the path of balance while continuing to listen, record, contemplate and observe. And, in actuality, she has been doing what she was afraid could never be accomplished. Isn't this a wonderful thing to know? Who *I* am loses importance when you begin to fully realize who *you* are. You are living, breathing, human entities, sparking with energy and focused on one goal—full realization of the Self and all the wonder and knowledge this contains. When you are committed to exploring the Self, you are ready to move forward, change what must be changed through honest observation and then let go of what does not serve you. I don't want you to quit your job, divorce your family, sell your house or move to a mountaintop. I want you to listen. That is all for now. Just listen. Take a breath. Ignore what distracts you and step into the light of a new wave of truth and enlightenment.

I can hear some of you now: "Not another path to enlightenment!" You may have heard these same teachings from teachers before. Similar truth has always been spoken since the beginning of time. When you make the choice to listen to such a teacher of truth, make sure that what is spoken gives you a sense of peace and that it is spoken with love, honor and great respect for the one who journeys. Do not become involved with those teachers who would bid you follow them without concern for your human life. If you choose to join a monastery and shave your head, do so because it is what the Self desires, not because the teacher has required it. Do not become a puppet in someone else's journey. Think for yourself, and know with certainty that following the truth of another is not the way to

Self-realization. Learn what they have to teach, but continue to seek your own enlightened truth. How will you know the difference? Acknowledge how it makes you feel to be in the presence of such truth. Do you ask and then receive the answers to your questions? Are you able to walk away and come back at will—your will? Are you given human dogma to follow, or allowed and encouraged to expand the wisdom of the Self? If you can speak honestly, without fear of reprisal, you are on the journey of Self-realization. I am simply a guidepost along the way, as are many. You are the star of the show. Never forget this simple statement. As the star, you bear the responsibility of seeking truth and making it your own. You must always keep to your own path in order to make your journey one of discovery and not one of recovery. It is your personal adventure. If you fall, dust yourself off and keep looking forward to what can and will be in your future, with your eyes wide open and your heart willing to receive. Come forth into the act of being until it is no longer an act but who you are in truth. You are the Self on a journey of discovery.

# AUTHOR'S NOTE

It was about midway through the completion of this book that I found myself deeply committed to more urgent family matters. The birth of my first grandchild and the ultimate decline of my ninety-year-old father were taking up most of my waking hours. Finishing this book took a distant place in priority. As days turned into weeks, I missed the time spent in contemplation of Mother's truths. While it was clearly apparent that family events were pulling me in several directions at once, I knew there were insights I needed to gain from these experiences, so I prayed for guidance and help in finding some answers.

In the shower one morning (my sanctuary for thinking, questioning and listening), Mother softly whispered to me, "It's about the Self." Okay. I think I've heard this somewhere before. It seemed that as many times as I had read over her messages about the Self I still failed to notice when I was given the opportunity to gain further understanding in this waking dream called life. Well, I was paying attention now. "It's about the Self," she said. The insights I gained began to tumble forth. I was being given the chance to experience firsthand life's ultimate cycle of birth through the eventual death of the body. I quickly jotted down these insights before going out the door to do what life demanded. *It's about the Self* is not just for quiet, meditative moments of At-One-Ment but for those moments filled with everyday distractions and responsibilities, as well as those of abundant joy. We are continually given the opportunity to begin and end each day with the Self as our guidepost, cheerleader, mentor and reality—in every interaction and reaction life offers—if we just pay attention.

As I went about my day loving the sweet softness of my baby granddaughter and holding the hand of my frightened and very frail father, I was reminded of those opportunities. In every moment I became more aware of the rare and special gift each one gave to my story. I appreciated and understood that the Self is about loving, giving and honoring these special moments, which need not be wasted by guilt or negative emotions. I recognized and was truly thankful for such insights that came from the center of God's heart into the center of mine. This connection is real, and I continually find a joyful peace and a thankful attitude toward life and all it brings. This is what it's about for me now—these moments in time in the presence of the Self, my God-center. With each breath I take, until my soul has been released, I will dwell in the light that shines from within the Self, the spark of Original Thought that illumes my path for yet another adventure.

I wish you peace and a life full of joyful "Ah-ha!" moments.

Namaste,
Judith